Tobacco

a global threat

Sir John Crofton MD (Camb)
Professor Emeritus of Respiratory Diseases and
Tuberculosis, University of Edinburgh

David Simpson
Director, International Agency on Tobacco
and Health

MACMILLAN

TALC

IATH
SWEDISH HEART
LUNG FOUNDATION

Macmillan Education
Between Towns Road, Oxford OX4 3PP
A division of Macmillan Publishers Limited
Companies and representatives throughout the world

www.macmillan-africa.com

ISBN 0 333 67081 7

Designed by Sue Clarke
Cover illustration courtesy of Still Pictures/James H. Karales

Commissioned photograph by Alan Thomas

Printed and bound in Malaysia

2006 2005 2004
10 9 8 7 6 5 4 3 2

Contents

Foreword

Nicotine addiction, through cigarette smoking and other tobacco use that it perpetuates, is the major cause of preventable deaths in our world. It is exceptional in that the income the cigarette companies and their shareholders receive is directly related to the number of people who become addicted to nicotine. Around half of those who become addicted will die of the many cancers and other diseases caused by tobacco. Moreover, parents' smoking can damage both their unborn babies and their children.

As a paediatrician I am particularly concerned with the worldwide targeting of cigarette promotion towards children and young women, the future mothers. Nicotine addiction is probably as difficult to overcome as addiction to cocaine. The younger a child becomes addicted the greater the damage done to health and the greater the difficulty and expense of curing the addiction.

Those who live in richer countries have more effective legal systems and community organisations which can resist the wealth of the tobacco companies intent on spreading nicotine addiction. This is not so in the 'resource poor' countries where most of the world's population live.

I sincerely hope this book may play a part in correcting that imbalance.

Professor David Morley CBE FRCP
Emeritus Professor of Tropical Child Health, University of London

Preface

Many of the poorer parts of the world are afflicted by two important epidemics. Tuberculosis has been causing misery and death for thousands of years. Sadly, with its alliance with the HIV virus, the disease is exploding in many countries. The newer epidemic is tobacco. This is now sweeping into poorer countries.

As the inhabitants of richer countries have begun to learn the grim lessons of suffering and death from tobacco, they are gradually abandoning the habit. Tobacco consumption is now decreasing in most industrialised countries. As a result, the multinational tobacco companies are more and more concentrating their skills and massive resources towards creating vast new markets in Asia, Africa and Latin America (as well as in Central and Eastern Europe). In some of these countries male smoking rates are already high or rising. Rates in women are at present mostly low. But, with skilled marketing, women could provide enormous future profits for tobacco companies. With the relatively long gap between starting to smoke and resulting disease and death, too many politicians and opinion-formers have not yet awoken to the threat.

The British charity Teaching-aids At Low Cost (TALC) specialises in providing books and material for medical schools in poor countries. In the early 1990s its Honorary Director, Professor David Morley, invited one of us (JC) and two colleagues (Norman Horne and Fred Miller) to write a book, *Clinical Tuberculosis*, for the use of health professionals in poor countries with very few resources. The book obviously fulfilled a real need: some 80,000 copies in two editions and 19 languages have been distributed in 125 countries.

Encouraged by this success, Professor Morley asked the present authors to produce a similar book for countries now so tragically threatened by the tobacco epidemic. We have written the book to help those in these countries who are trying to save their populations from this future misery and death. The book is therefore primarily for activists and advocates in the tobacco field. But it should also be useful for a wider audience, including health professionals, journalists, politicians, and all responsible people concerned about human health and welfare, especially that of women and children.

We have drawn both on our professional knowledge of smoking-related diseases and on our many years' experience, national and international, of campaigning on tobacco. With increasing leadership, both from the World Health Organization and from many international non-governmental organisations, the time is becoming much more favourable for controlling the epidemic. But we must not underestimate the skills and power of the opposition – the tobacco industry and its allies.

In writing the book we have been able to adapt much of the material used by one of the authors (DS) in preparing his book *Doctors and Tobacco* written for the European Forum of Medical Associations and the World Health Organization. The present book is complementary, being addressed to a different and wider readership. We are grateful for permission to use a number of illustrations from that book. Our book is also, we hope, complementary to the excellent book *Tobacco Control and Prevention* published by the International Union against Tuberculosis and Lung Disease (IUATLD). Again we are grateful for permission to reproduce in an Appendix some of the joint WHO/IUATLD questionnaires. We also thank the Editor of the journal *Tobacco Control* and the relevant artists etc. for permission to use a number of illustrations which appeared in that journal.

We thank Dr Eileen Crofton, former Medical Director of ASH Scotland, and Dr Amanda Amos for suggestions, in particular regarding the chapter on women.

We owe our deepest thanks to Elizabeth Ann Pretty for preparing draft after draft, and amendment after amendment, of the text and for taking such an immense interest in the work. Anne-Marie Guillemot of the International Agency on Tobacco and Health (IATH) gave much assistance over the illustrations. Amanda Sandford of ASH (UK) was a frequent help in tracing references and information regarding the health effects of tobacco. Philip Boys has done a wonderful job in finalising our draft and some of the illustrations and in designing the cover.

We are most grateful for the continuing encouragement of Professor David Morley, who made many useful suggestions on earlier drafts of the text, and for the ongoing interest and help of Shirley Hamber of our publishers. It was a great pleasure to work with Sheila Jones, publishing editor, who was unfailingly helpful.

We are proud that the book is sponsored not only by TALC but also by the IUATLD and the Swedish Heart Lung Association.

Financial support

We were anxious that the book should be as cheap as possible. For this we needed substantial financial subsidy (the authors take no fees or royalties). We are most grateful to the following for their generous contributions:

Chest Heart and Stroke Scotland, Christian Aid, The Swedish Heart Lung Association, The Danish Lung Association, Australian Tuberculosis and Chest Association, Community Health and Anti-Tuberculosis Association (New South Wales, Australia), Victorian Tuberculosis and Lung Association (Australia), and WESTCARE (Australia).

We also thank other donors whose contributions may have reached us too late to include in this list.

John Crofton   David Simpson

Acknowledgements

Acknowledgements for illustrations appear in the figure captions.

. The publishers have made every effort to trace the copyright holders, but if they have inadvertently overlooked any, they will be pleased to make the necessary arrangements at the first opportunity.

1 | The Tobacco Epidemic: the present world situation

Global trends in tobacco deaths

> With current smoking patterns, 500 million people alive today will eventually be killed by tobacco use. More than half of these are now children and teenagers. By 2030 tobacco is expected to be the single biggest cause of death worldwide.
>
> World Bank, 1999

In the world as a whole, tobacco already kills 1 in 10 adults. By 2030 it is expected to kill 1 in 6, or more than 10 million deaths a year. At least 7 in 10 of these deaths will be in low-income or middle-income countries.

A survey in 1990 showed that in 44 industrialised countries, smoking caused an average of 24% of all male deaths – but 35% of deaths in middle age (35–69). It also caused 7% of all female deaths overall. In the USA, where a high proportion of women smoke, it was 17%.

The average loss of life in smokers is 8 years. For those who die in middle age, it is as much as 22 years.

About half of all regular smokers are eventually killed by smoking.

Global numbers of smokers

- About 47% of men and 12% of women smoke (WHO, 1997).
- Although smoking rates in high-income countries are now declining, on present global trends the number of smokers is expected to rise from 1.1 billion to 1.6 billion by 2025.
- In high-income countries most smokers start smoking in their teens. In poorer countries they mostly start in their early twenties, but the peak age of starting to smoke is getting younger.
- In most countries there is already more smoking among the poor than the rich. Smoking makes the poor poorer – money is spent on tobacco instead of on food or other family needs. In short, their health is doubly threatened.

Comment on global figures

These basic figures for deaths due to smoking are indeed grim. We must also remember that very large numbers of smokers suffer years of misery before they die. Moreover, smoking by mothers during pregnancy may cause long-term physical and intellectual damage to their babies (Chapter 3). Smoking by both parents may cause illness in their children (Chapter 3). Children of smokers are more likely to become smokers themselves and so die like their parents (see Chapter 6).

Research has shown that breathing other people's smoke may cause cancer and other health problems (Chapter 3). In many countries this has increased demands for smoke-free public places, transport and work-places. This in turn makes smoking less fashionable. Fewer people take up smoking and more smokers want to quit (Chapter 3). We discuss the importance of this in tobacco control (Chapter 10) and in campaigning (Chapter 12).

In many countries the low numbers of women smokers are a tempting future market for tobacco companies (Chapter 5). The companies are making huge efforts to recruit these customers (Chapter 9). Campaigning to prevent that recruitment is vitally important (Chapters 10 and 12).

Regional variations in smoking

Figure 1.1, based on the World Bank Report (1999), shows smoking rates for adults and total numbers of smokers by World Bank Region. Note that a high proportion of the world's smokers (48%) live in the East Asia/Pacific and Eastern Europe/Central Asia Regions, where smoking rates for men are very high. Note also the relatively low rates for women in Eastern Asia and Pacific; Middle East and North Africa; and South Asia. Unfortunately the rates for women are rising in some of these countries. (For more details on rates and trends for women see Chapter 5.)

As mentioned above, in higher income countries most smokers start in childhood. To replace those dying from smoking, tobacco companies have to recruit new smokers. The companies deny that they advertise to children. They often now claim that they aim to protect children. 'Smoking is an adult activity. Wait until you are grown up.' What a good way to challenge children to take up this 'adult activity'! (See Chapter 6.)

As adult smoking develops in poorer countries, more and more children copy adults. They begin to smoke at an even earlier age.

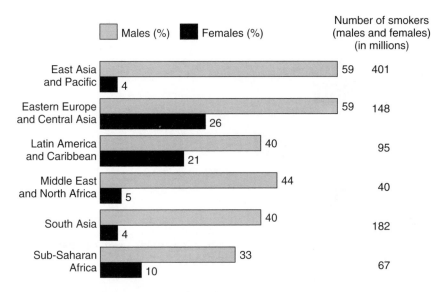

Figure 1.1 Regional patterns of smoking.
(Adapted from World Bank report (World Bank, 1999), using estimates from WHO (WHO, 1997) for adults over 15. **Note:** Figures for South Asia combine figures for smoking of manufactured cigarettes and *bidis* (small hand-rolled cigarettes in a leaf wrapper))

Smoking and income

Country income

Figure 1.2 summarises smoking rates and numbers of smokers according to country income. Many high-income countries are showing continuous falls in the number of smokers (WHO, 1997). On the other hand, in many of these countries, there has been a recent reversal: a disturbing rise in smoking among young women. However, 82% of the world's smokers now live in low-income or middle-income countries. In these countries WHO reports an *increase* in cigarette consumption of about 1.4% per year.

Personal income

In most high-income countries, smoking rates in men have fallen among richer, better-educated people, but remain high among the poor. Recent research in many middle- and lower-income countries has also found higher smoking rates among the poor (World Bank, 1999). In India richer

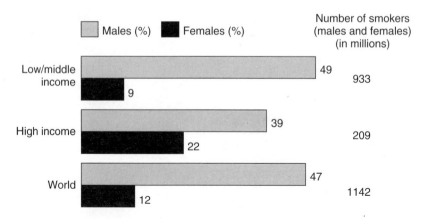

Figure 1.2 Smoking rates according to income of countries. (Adapted from World Bank report (World Bank, 1999), using estimates from WHO (WHO, 1997) for adults over 15)

people tend to smoke manufactured cigarettes; poorer people smoke *bidis* (small hand-rolled cigarettes in a leaf wrapper). In South Asia as a whole, about half of all male smokers smoke *bidis*.

Smokeless (oral) tobacco

In addition to cigarettes, WHO calculates that some 400 million people, chiefly in Central and South Asia, consume smokeless (oral) tobacco. Smokeless tobacco has its own health risks. It probably causes some 100,000 cancers a year in men and 50,000 in women. In some of these countries consumption is increasing (see Chapter 4).

Conclusions

- The fairly steady falls in smoking, following concerted action in many high-income countries are encouraging. This fall is due to many factors. These include: action by doctors and other health professionals (Chapter 8); increasing help in quitting smoking (Chapter 7); changes in public opinion, with greater awareness of health risks (Chapter 12); legal action (Chapter 11); in many countries, the development of at least some form of national tobacco control programme (Chapter 10). But recent rises in smoking rates in young women are causing concern.

- On the other hand, there is an alarming increase in smoking in many poorer countries. This is due to intensive marketing by tobacco companies (see Chapter 9). Rising income in some Asian countries may also be contributing.
- The relatively low smoking rates in women in many of these countries provide a vast potential market for tobacco companies. The companies are making great efforts to exploit that market (see Chapter 5).
- These trends, unless they can be stopped, will result in enormous future increases in misery, death and economic loss (see Chapter 2).
- Establishing effective national and international tobacco control is therefore an urgent priority. Fortunately, this has now been recognised by the World Health Organization (see Chapter 10).

References

World Bank. 1999. Curbing the epidemic. Governments and the economics of tobacco control. Washington: World Bank. ISBN 0-8213-4519-2.
An excellent, short and readable account of the world tobacco situation. Covers global and regional trends in tobacco use, health consequences, and the economics both of tobacco and of tobacco control.

World Health Organization. 1997.Tobacco or health. A global status report. Geneva: WHO. ISBN 92-4-156184-X
A thorough review of global consumption, smoking rates, tobacco industry and national tobacco control action by country up to 1995–96. Mainly valuable as a reference book.

2 | The Menace of Tobacco to Health

Worldwide, tobacco is one of the most important causes of disability, suffering and premature death. In many countries it is the most important cause. Yet almost alone among causes of ill-health, it is one that can in principle be completely prevented (see Chapter 1).

> **Why tobacco is a unique public health problem**
> Tobacco is a uniquely dangerous consumer product, lethal even when used exactly as intended by the manufacturers.
> - It is always dangerous, not just when it is used in excess or abused (as is the case with many other preventable causes of ill-health).
> - Its smoke contains thousands of chemicals. Many of these are known poisons. Some damage blood vessels, others cause cancer. They can harm every part of the body.
> - It is highly addictive to many of its consumers.
> - It is actively and energetically promoted by one of the world's most powerful industries.
> - Its use not only harms those who consume it, but also other people exposed to their smoke.

Tobacco smoke

More than 4000 chemicals have been identified in tobacco smoke. Many are poisonous, some are radioactive. More than 40 are known to cause cancer. These are particularly concentrated in **tar**, the brown sticky liquid that condenses from the smoke. The reason tobacco produces so many different chemicals is related to the very high temperatures (up to 900°C) generated in the glowing tip when the smoker inhales.

Nicotine is the main cause of physical addiction. (Experts conclude that it is at least as addictive as heroin.) Thanks to the efficiency of the lungs and blood vessels, nicotine reaches the brain within 7 seconds of starting to smoke. Nicotine increases the heart rate and blood pressure so that the heart needs more oxygen. As a result, the effects of nicotine may be one of the causes of sudden death in middle-aged heavy smokers. The effects of nicotine are made worse by carbon monoxide from the smoke.

Carbon monoxide pushes oxygen out of the blood's red cells. So tissues, including the heart, get less oxygen – though the heart needs more oxygen because of the nicotine.

Smoking also increases hardening of the artery walls (atherosclerosis) and makes blood clot more easily. Both may block a heart artery and cause part of heart muscle to die. Smoking also tends to increase blood cholesterol. High cholesterol is part of the cause of coronary artery disease (ischaemic heart disease, heart attacks) and stroke.

Some 85% of the smoke in a room is usually **sidestream smoke** from the burning tip of the cigarette. This is what a non-smoker usually inhales. Many toxins occur in higher concentrations in sidestream smoke than in the smoke directly inhaled from the cigarette.

Smoke from pipes and cigars has a higher tar content than cigarette smoke. Most lifelong pipe and cigar smokers do not inhale, so they take in less tar than cigarette smokers. In some countries cigar smoking is again being promoted as a fashionable, alternative to cigarettes – indeed, it is often perceived as a 'healthier' alternative. In fact, both pipe and cigar smokers are liable to mouth and throat cancer, and a recent study has also shown a significant risk of chronic obstructive pulmonary disease (chronic bronchitis and emphysema), and ischaemic heart disease (Iribarren et al., 1999).

Smoking related diseases (Figure 2.1)
- Major killers
  - Coronary artery disease (ischaemic heart disease, or 'heart attacks')
  - Chronic obstructive pulmonary disease (COPD, including chronic bronchitis and emphysema)
  - Lung cancer
  - Other cancers: Mouth, throat, bladder, kidneys, pancreas, oesophagus (gullet), stomach, liver, myeloid and monocytic leukaemia (blood cancer)
- Blood vessels
  - Peripheral vascular disease (usually in the legs)
  - Stroke (brain)
  - Aortic aneurysm (ballooning in aorta, the main artery)
- Pneumonia and other lung conditions
- Others
  - Hip fractures
  - Cataracts
  - Gum infections
- Effects on reproduction

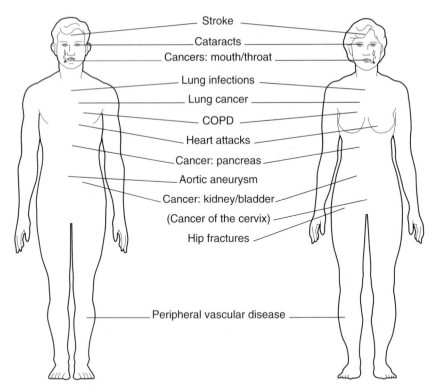

Figure 2.1 Principal diseases caused by smoking: COPD (Chronic Obstructive Pulmonary Disease) is also known as 'chronic bronchitis and emphysema'. Cancer of the cervix is in brackets because of certain problems – see text.

Evidence on smoking as a cause of disease

Early solid evidence came from **case-control** or **retrospective studies**, such as Doll and Hill's 1950 study of lung cancer (Doll and Hill, 1950). Smoking rates in patients with a disease such as lung cancer (the 'cases') were compared with smoking rates in a group of patients of the same age and social class but with diseases that were unlikely to be caused by smoking (the 'controls').

Many **prospective** studies followed later. In these, the smoking and other habits of a group in the population are recorded in great detail. The group is then followed up for a number of years. Deaths from different diseases can then be compared with smoking habits previously recorded.

A classic study of British doctors tracked for 40 years is a good example of this strategy (see Figures 2.2 and 2.3). It has not only demonstrated the extent to which smoking causes diseases, it has also shown that for most such diseases quitting smoking leads to a rapid decrease in risk.

Similar conclusions have been reached from studies based on comparing statistics of tobacco consumption with smoking-related deaths. When smoking rates rise in a country, smoking-related mortality rises 20–30 years later. When tobacco consumption falls, after an interval the smoking-related mortality also starts to fall (See Figure 5.1 on page 35).

The tobacco industry is fond of saying that projections of future smoking deaths worldwide are solely based on studies of smokers in the West. This is not true. Indeed, the largest study of tobacco deaths ever undertaken was done in China. A retrospective study of one million deaths and a prospective study of 200,000 adults, concluded that in China at present 1 in 4 deaths in smokers are due to tobacco, and that this will rise to 1 in 2 as the epidemic develops. Tobacco will kill one in every three young men alive today – about 100 million people (Liu et al., 1998).

Preliminary results of a major survey in India show that the hazards are already substantial. The full results, when published, seem likely to parallel findings elsewhere. In the long term, 1 in 2 of all persistent smokers will die of smoking-related disease.

The patterns of smoking-related diseases differ somewhat from country to country. In Western countries deaths from cardiovascular disease are comparatively the most numerous. In China chronic obstructive respiratory disease is the most prominent and cardiovascular disease is less prominent. In both India and China smoking seems very important in increasing the risk of pulmonary tuberculosis, a major disease in both countries (Peto and Lopez, 2001).

Finally, **laboratory evidence** has also shown that tobacco smoke or tar can produce cancer in animals.

Cardiovascular (heart and blood vessel) diseases

Coronary (or ischaemic) heart disease

In many industrialised countries, coronary heart disease is one of the commonest causes of death. In men under 45, the majority of heart attacks have been shown to be due to smoking. At all ages the smoker's risk is 10–15 times that of non-smokers.

In countries that have taken appropriate action (such as cutting smoking, improving monitoring and treatment), death rates are now falling. In many developing countries, however, rates are rising.

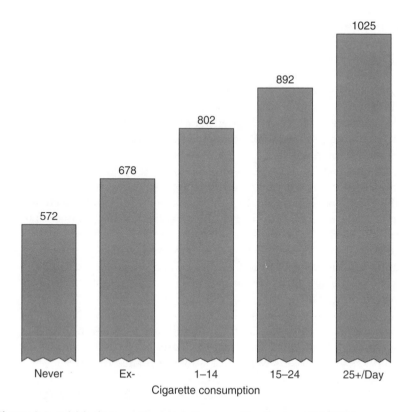

Figure 2.2 British doctors 40-year follow-up. Deaths per 100,000 from ischaemic heart disease in relation to cigarette habit. (Adapted from: Doll et al. 1994 BMJ 309: 901–911, with kind permission from the BMJ Publishing Group)

There are many causes of heart disease, including high blood pressure, raised blood cholesterol, diet, obesity, lack of exercise, diabetes and genetic factors – the more of these that are present, the higher the risk. But the most important and preventable cause is cigarette smoking (Figure 2.2).

Benefits of stopping smoking

- The risk of a **heart attack** is halved (or more) within a year of stopping. Then it slowly declines still further.
- Stopping **after a heart attack** can halve the chance of suffering another attack. Stopping is particularly important for people with other risk factors.

- **Stroke** (caused by clotting or rupture in the blood vessels of the brain). The death rate from stroke is higher in smokers, and increases with number of cigarettes smoked. After stopping, the death rate decreases significantly within 2 years. It reaches the risk for non-smokers after 5 years.
- **Peripheral vascular disease** /atherosclerosis (hardening and narrowing of arteries to legs). This initially makes walking painful. Later it may cause gangrene, requiring amputation of one or both legs (in England, 2000 people a year lose limbs from this cause alone). Of patients with peripheral vascular disease 90% are smokers. Diabetecs are particularly at risk.
- **Aortic aneurysm** (ballooning of the large artery that runs through the chest and abdomen). Aneurysms, which are more common among smokers, can be lethal if they burst.
- **Women on oral contraceptives** ('the birth control pill') have a higher risk of heart attacks, stroke or cerebral haemorrhage if they smoke. The risk is highest in older age groups. After stopping smoking the risk from all these sources immediately falls.

A case of angina pectoris

Mr Caposi, a lorry driver, had started smoking at the age of 16. He smoked fairly steadily during his long hours of driving. He had his first cigarette when he woke in the morning. In his early forties he began to find that when he did much heavy lifting or longer walking he felt a strangling feeling of heavy pressure in his upper chest. The feeling sometimes spread to his left arm and hand. It occurred especially after a meal and in cold weather. It quickly stopped if he rested. He went to his doctor who diagnosed angina and gave him a treatment to take when he got an attack. Each time this quickly relieved the symptoms. But he began to have attacks after less and less exercise. Mr Caposi's labour union provided health insurance. He was referred to a heart specialist who investigated his damaged coronary arteries. He was then referred to a cardiac surgeon. The surgeon said he could do a repair operation on the arteries of his heart but it would be much more certainly successful if Mr Caposi could stop smoking. Mr Caposi realised that his heart problem could kill him without the operation so, with the help of a smoking counsellor, he managed to stop. The operation was successful. He lost his symptoms and managed to return to work. He gave up smoking permanently. He is still working.

COMMENT Mr Caposi was fortunate that he was able to have full modern treatment. Without it he would have had worsening and more disabling symptoms. At any time he could have had a fatal heart attack. As he had stopped smoking, this was now less probable.

A typical 'heart attack' (myocardial infarction)

Mrs Dordrecht was the daughter of a rich merchant and had married a successful businessman. Like many well-off young women in her country, she had started smoking as an adolescent. She became a heavy smoker. Her husband also smoked. They both took little exercise. They had servants. They ate a rich diet. Mrs Dordrecht had three children in the first ten years of her married life. At the age of 45, after a heavy evening meal, she suddenly felt a severe pain over both sides of her upper chest. It spread upwards to her jaw and down to her left arm. She felt weak and nauseated. Her husband called the doctor. The doctor immediately diagnosed a heart attack and sent her straight into the coronary care unit in a private hospital. After being dangerously ill for the first few hours, Mrs Dordrecht gradually improved. She had been too ill to smoke. The specialist told her that she should stop smoking permanently. This would greatly reduce the chances of a second attack. But Mrs Dordrecht was used to having her own way. She was used to a comfortable life. For her a comfortable life included smoking. She failed to take the doctor's advice. A few months later she had a second attack after a heavy meal. She died twenty minutes later – before the doctor arrived.

A sudden unexpected death

Mr Fortescu was a highly successful academic who was having a brilliant career. As a student he had become a heavy smoker. He continued to smoke while he worked. He knew about the risks of smoking but he had few smoking symptoms. He never tried to quit. At the age of 48, one evening he was to hold a dinner party at his home for a foreign visitor to his department. He went to open the door for one of the visitors. As he did so, he suddenly fell down dead.

COMMENT Although, as noted in this chapter, smoking is not the only cause of coronary heart disease, the majority of sudden fatal heart attacks in middle age are due to smoking. Some of these patients can be saved by immediate first aid action.

Peripheral vascular disease

Mr Kulu was a labourer in a large town. He had started smoking as a boy and continued to smoke heavily. He had a smoker's cough. He often got chest colds in the winter. At the age of 50 he began to have a cramping pain in his calf muscles when he walked for any great distance. The pain soon stopped if he rested. Gradually the pain came on after shorter and shorter walks. He had to give up work. He began to notice that some of his toes on the right foot were becoming a little brown and shrivelled. He went to a doctor who referred him to a charity hospital. The surgeon there told him that the cause was disease in the arteries of the legs. The surgeon said that this was due to smoking. If Mr Kulu did not stop he would have to have his right leg amputated, as gangrene was starting in his toes. An operation could be done to improve the blood flow to his right leg. But it was much more likely to succeed if he could stop smoking. Mr Kulu did try to quit, but without success. The surgeon did do the operation but it failed to help. Mr Kulu had to have his right leg amputated. Soon the same thing started in his left leg. This had also to be amputated. He still could not stop smoking. Eventually a fatal attack of pneumonia, resulting from his smoking, put him out of his misery.

COMMENT This disease is almost always due to smoking. These patients seem usually to be very severely addicted to their nicotine. They often have the greatest difficulty in quitting smoking – even when they are faced with a possible limb amputation. Perhaps this is because some have successfully stopped in the early stages of the disease; and therefore it is only the most addicted smokers who go on to the final stages of this horrible disease.

Lung diseases

Chronic obstructive pulmonary disease (COPD)

COPD is also known as chronic bronchitis and emphysema.

In most industrialised countries COPD is one of the three major killers in adult life. Like cancer and heart disease, COPD mainly occurs in smokers. Death rates are directly related to the cigarettes smoked (Figure 2.3).

Atmospheric pollution from industry adds to the risks, as do open fires and charcoal stoves in houses with no chimneys – where rooms may be full of smoke from cooking and heating.

Patients start with a 'smoker's cough', often at first only in the winter or wet season. Over the years they may become wheezy. Things often get worse ('exacerbations') after a cold, leading perhaps to pneumonia. With time they become more and more breathless. This may lead to heart failure due to the difficulty in pumping blood through damaged lungs. The late stages are very miserable, with severe breathlessness and frequent exacerbations. (See stories below.)

The benefits of quitting

In younger patients, cough and wheeze will decrease or even disappear. Lung function may improve. In middle-aged or older people, cough will improve, or even disappear, and there are usually fewer chest illnesses. Lung function will usually not improve, but it will now decrease at the

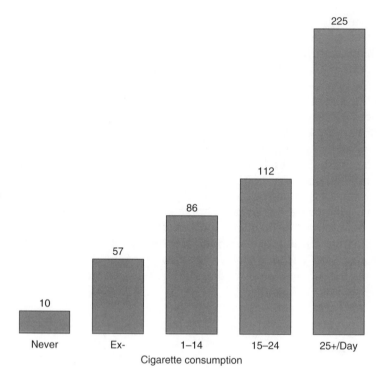

Figure 2.3 British doctors 40-year follow-up. Deaths per 100,000 from chronic obstructive lung disease in relation to cigarette habit. (Adapted from: Doll et al. 1994 BMJ 309: 901–911, with kind permission from the BMJ Publishing Group)

normal rate for advancing age. (If smoking had continued it would have got worse much more quickly: Figure 2.4).

Pneumonia and lung infections

There is much evidence that lung infections occur more frequently in smokers. This is true at all ages, including childhood and adolescence (see Chapter 6).

A typical story of COPD

Mr Zatorski worked in a factory in a large industrial town. Like most of his friends, he had started smoking cigarettes as an adolescent. As a young man his winter colds often 'went to his chest' with severe cough which lasted weeks. He had been a keen footballer, but in his late 20s found he was getting too breathless for severe exertion. As he got older the cough became more continuous and even worse in winter.

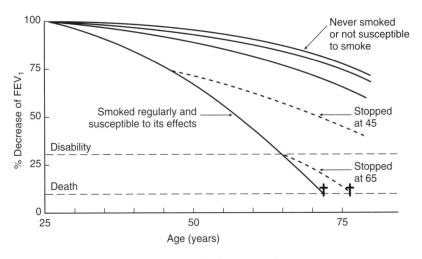

Figure 2.4 Decrease of lung function with age. Effect of tobacco smoking. Note much steeper decrease in smokers and benefits from quitting. FEV is short for Forced Expiratory Volume in 1 second. It is the commonest method used for measuring lung function. (Reproduced from the report of the Royal College of Physicians of London, 1983: 27)

There was often pus in his sputum (phlegm). His breathing was often wheezy. His winter 'chest colds' got more severe. He had to have more and more time off work. His doctor advised him to stop smoking. He made one or two attempts. But all his fellow workers smoked. He never managed to stop for more than a day or two. He got steadily more breathless. He finally had to stop work permanently. He could no longer manage the heavy lifting. His wife got some part-time work but the family became much poorer. He found difficulty in climbing the stairs. Several times he had to go into hospital with a severe attack. He still could not stop smoking. Soon he became too breathless to leave his house. It was even an effort to get out of bed and dress. Finally, at the age of 55, he was admitted to hospital with a severe chest infection and pneumonia. In spite of oxygen and antibiotics he died in a few hours.

COMMENT This is a very common story. The grim effect of smoking is often made worse in industrial towns by fog and atmospheric pollution. Research has shown that the later invalid life can be prolonged by using oxygen every day at home, but this is very expensive and not available to many patients, particularly in poor countries. The quality of life of course still remains very poor. The progressive damage to the lungs can also give rise to 'pulmonary heart failure'.

An 'emphysema' story

Miss Capoc had been a very intelligent child. She did very well at school, and then went on to university. In her country smoking had been taken up by many intelligent girls who were beginning to enter professional jobs. They felt it was a sign of the increasing sophistication and liberation of women. She did well at university and later became a lecturer. She continued to smoke heavily. One year she had quite a severe attack of bronchitis. Her doctor gave her antibiotics and she gradually recovered. After that she had very little cough but became more and more breathless. She never married. In her mid 50s she became so breathless that she had to retire early. She had tried to stop smoking several times but was so addicted that she found it impossible. Later, she could not do her shopping or housework and was confined to her home. She had got emphysema (the gradual breaking down of the air sacs in the lung through which oxygen enters the bloodstream). With her small pension and help from her family, she was able to afford some home help. Finally, at the age of 58, after years of breathless misery, a sudden chest infection was quickly fatal.

COMMENT This is a less common way smoking can kill. There is often much overlap between the mainly bronchitic illness shown by Mr Zatorski, with much cough and wheeze, and the grimly long and increasingly breathless illness of Miss Capoc. Miss Capoc's illness also shows the tragic type of severe tobacco addiction, so difficult to break even by a highly intelligent woman. Fortunately, with modern nicotine replacement therapy (see Chapter 7) it is becoming easier to help such patients to quit smoking.

Lung cancer

Lung cancer was once relatively unusual. However, as smoking became more widespread, so did lung cancer. About 9 out of 10 cases of lung cancer are due to smoking.

There has been a major epidemic of lung cancer in all industrialised countries. In countries that have taken effective action, this rate has now fallen in men but continues to rise among women (who generally took up smoking later). In some countries, lung cancer mortality in women has now overtaken that of breast cancer, i.e. has become the most common cause of cancer death.

Both male and female lung cancer rates are still rising steeply in many countries of central and Eastern Europe. They are also now beginning to rise in many lower income countries in which smoking has increased. In Shanghai, where smoking has been common for a long time, lung cancer death rates among men are similar to those of men in many western countries.

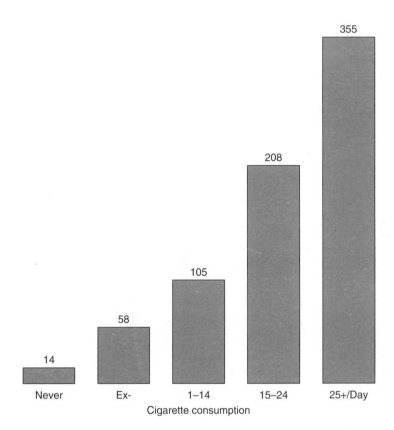

Figure 2.5 British doctors 40-year follow-up. Deaths per 100,000 from lung cancer in relation to cigarette habit. (Adapted from: Doll et al. 1994 BMJ 309: 901–911, with kind permission from the BMJ Publishing Group)

Prevention is the answer to this common and lethal disease, as treatment is relatively unsuccessful.

Figure 2.5 shows the death rates of the 40-year follow-up of British doctors according to the number of cigarettes they had smoked a day. Figure 2.6 shows the smaller but important effect of pipe and cigar smoking. Figure 2.7 shows the reduction in risk in those who quit. It has been concluded that 90% of lung cancer is due to smoking.

Lung cancer affects patients in various ways. We show some of these in the following stories.

A common story
Mr Weng was an office clerk in a large seaport in Asia. When he was very young, cigarettes were imported from abroad for the use of the

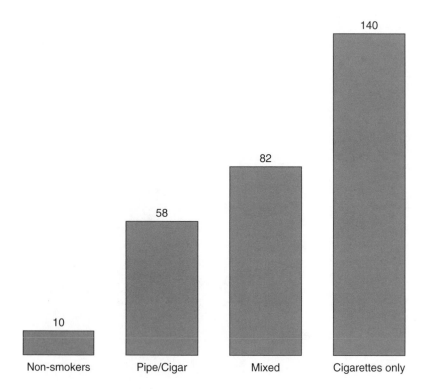

Figure 2.6 Lung cancer deaths per 100,000 per year for British male doctors 1951–71. (Adapted from: Doll and Peto 1976 BMJ ii:1525, with kind permission from the BMJ Publishing Group)

many Europeans and Americans working there. The habit spread to local workers, especially the better paid in factories and offices. Mr Weng started smoking in his early 20s and was soon smoking heavily. Gradually over the years he began to get a 'smoker's cough' and a little breathless. At the age of 55 one winter the cough became worse. He became more breathless. He began to feel tired and unwell. He lost a little weight. One morning when he coughed he noticed there were streaks of blood in his sputum (phlegm). This happened over several days so he went to a doctor. The blood made the doctor suspect either tuberculosis or lung cancer. He sent Mr Weng to a specialist at the large local hospital. No tubercle bacilli were found in his sputum. X-ray showed a large shadow near the root of the right lung. Examination of his bronchi (lung air tubes) with a bronchoscope showed a cancerous growth in the main bronchus to his right lung. The doctor felt a small lump behind the inner end of his right collarbone. This was shown to be a spread of the cancer to a 'lymph

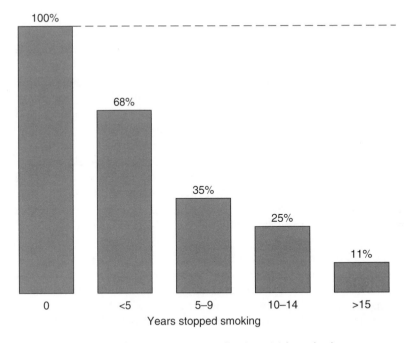

Figure 2.7 Decrease in lung cancer mortality in British male doctors (1951–71) Note that the mortality decreases steadily according to the number of years doctors had stopped smoking. (Adapted from: Doll and Peto 1976 BMJ ii:1525, with kind permission from the BMJ Publishing Group)

node' there. This meant that an operation to remove the lung cancer could not cure him. The cancer had already spread to the lymph node and probably further into his body. Treatment could only help to keep him as comfortable as possible. Mr Weng got steadily iller, lost his appetite, lost weight; his cough was very severe. He died 6 months later.

COMMENT Sadly, this is an all too common story. Although much research is now being done on other treatments, such as radiotherapy and anti-cancer drugs, so far the results are still poor. Many lung cancer patients die within a year of diagnosis. Even with the best available modern treatment, only a small minority are still alive 5 years after diagnosis.

A dangerous 'pneumonia'

Mrs Tsuli was a schoolteacher. When she was young, few women in her country smoked. But when she was at her teacher training college, smoking became popular as a sign that educated women were now becoming more 'liberated', sophisticated, and 'Western'. Although she did well in her career, became an assistant head teacher, and married happily, she continued to smoke. She began to have attacks of bronchitis, which kept her off work, sometimes for several weeks. She got rather more breathless. At the age of 48 one of her bronchitis attacks went on to severe pneumonia with fever and pain in her left chest. This was treated with antibiotics. The fever subsided but she continued to cough. She still had pain in her left chest and felt generally unwell. Her doctor sent her to hospital. X-rays showed a shadow in her left lower lung. It also showed that there was a gap in the bone shadow of one of her left ribs where she had had the pain. Examination with a bronchoscope confirmed a cancer. The obstruction of the bronchus by the cancer had led to infection beyond. This had caused her pneumonia.

The gap in the rib showed that cancer cells had spread there through the bloodstream and were destroying part of the rib. Again, no curative treatment was possible. Mrs Tsuli died a few months later. She spent much of the last few months of her life trying to persuade all her smoking friends to quit and so to save them from the same fate.

COMMENT In her later years Mrs Tsuli did come to know that cigarettes were dangerous. Like many smokers she felt psychologically 'It can't happen to me' – until it did. To her great credit, she felt that no one could help her but she could help her friends to avoid the same tragedy.

One of the lucky few
Mr Subramanyan was a skilled worker in a large factory in a rapidly developing country. When he was young, cigarette smoking had begun to be popular. It had spread rapidly among young men of his age. Apart from a mild smoker's cough, worse in winter, for many years he had had no obvious ill effects. His country still had a big problem with tuberculosis. The owners of his factory were good employers. In order to help to diagnose tuberculosis early, both for the sake of any patients and to prevent the spread of the disease among other workers, the owners arranged for an X-ray survey of all their workers. Though he had no important symptoms Mr Subramanyan was surprised to be recalled after the X-ray. The doctor told him that there was a small shadow in his lung X-ray which needed investigation. To cut a long story short, investigation showed no evidence of TB. The small persistent shadow was found to be a slow-growing type of lung cancer. There was no evidence of cancer spread elsewhere. A surgeon removed

the lobe of his lung containing the cancer. He got over the operation well. He turned out to be one of the very few lucky ones who was alive 5 years later.

COMMENT Mr Subramanyan was indeed lucky. The cancer was picked up at an early stage. It had not spread either locally or in another part of his body. He was rapidly sent for skilled diagnosis and skilled surgery – in many regions not available for most patients. Few patients are as lucky as Mr Subramanyan.

A more unusual story

Mr Musa was one of two partners in a small business. He and his partner had both been heavy cigarette smokers for many years. They knew about the dangers of tobacco. He had a mild smoker's cough and had had several attacks of bronchitis. His doctor had advised him to stop smoking. He had made a number of unsuccessful attempts. When Mr Musa was 61 he was on holiday when he rather suddenly began to feel unsteady. He had difficulty in keeping his balance. Something was obviously seriously wrong. So his wife took him home. He went straight to his doctor, who referred him immediately to a specialist. The specialist admitted him to hospital at once. Mr Musa rapidly became more drowsy.

Investigations showed there was some damage at the base of the brain in a vital area that controls many body functions, including balance. He became unconscious. He died within a couple of weeks. As the diagnosis was uncertain, his wife gave permission for a post-mortem examination. The pathologist found that there was a small tumour, about the size of a pea, in the expected area of the brain. In one of his bronchial tubes there was a small lung cancer which had not shown up on the first X-ray. It had caused him no obvious problem. It had seeded cancer cells through his bloodstream to his brain.

Even this sad tragedy did not persuade his business partner to stop smoking to avoid the same fate. A year or two later, one morning he got a sudden pain in his chest. He immediately thought 'This may be a heart attack'. He knew that heart attacks could be due to smoking. He stopped smoking at once. The pain very shortly disappeared. He was proud at having quit and felt so much better for doing so that he never returned to his cigarettes. He is now in his 80s, well for his age, and still proud of his non-smoking state.

COMMENT Lung cancer can spread to any part of the body. So occasionally it first shows through one of these 'secondary' cancers. It may show, as in this patient, as a brain tumour. Or it may show as a bone tumour causing local pain.

Other cancers

Cancers of the mouth and throat

Cigarettes, pipes and cigars increase the risk for all cancers of the mouth and throat by similar amounts. The risk increases with the number of cigarettes smoked. Heavy smokers are at 20–30 times greater risk than non-smokers.

Combining smoking with heavy drinking of alcohol makes for an even greater risk (it accounts for about 3 out of 4 cancers in this area). For cancers of the larynx, it is even higher – 9 out of 10 (Simpson, 1999).

Pancreatic cancers

The risk for men smoking over 20 cigarettes a day is 5 times that of non-smokers; for women 6 times. After quitting, the risk is back to that of non-smokers by 10 years (Mack et al., 1986).

Bladder and kidney cancers

Smoking is one of the contributory factors. A British study found male smokers were 70% and female smokers 40% more likely to contract these cancers than non-smokers (Cartwright et al., 1983).

Myeloid and monocytic leukaemia (blood cancer)

A large-scale study of US veterans showed excess risk of 53% for current smokers and 39% for ex-smokers (Kinlen and Rogot, 1988).

Cervical cancer of the uterus (womb)

Many studies show roughly a doubling of risk for women who smoke compared with those who are non-smokers. (However, the evidence here is not conclusive. This cancer is associated with certain types of human papilloma virus, and infection is more likely in women who have had multiple sexual partners. If they also have higher smoking rates, the relationship is confounded (confused) (Doll, 1996)).

Cancers of the stomach

Smoking is probably a minor influence – the more important causes seem to be in the diet. However, smokers may tend to eat a more dangerous or less protective diet, and smoking is known to affect uptake of nutrients (see Doll, 1996). *Helicobacter* infection is probably also a factor.

Other health effects of tobacco

Osteoporosis and hip fractures

Women who smoke are more likely to develop osteoporosis (weaker bones) after the menopause, putting them at greater risk of hip and other bone fractures. Smoking is known to inhibit calcium take-up throughout life, which may partly account for this finding (ASH, 1995; Wald and Hackshaw, 1996).

Eyesight

Cataracts (clouding of the lens) of the eye. People who smoke 20 or more cigarettes a day have twice the risk of developing cataracts as non-smokers (Napier, 1995a).

Macular degeneration (damage to the 'seeing cells' in the retina at the back of the eye), a common cause of blindness in older people, is 2–5 times more common in smokers than in non-smokers (Mitchell et al. 1999).

Gum infections

Gum infections around teeth, and tooth loss, are also more common among smokers.

Reproduction and fertility

Smoking can damage reproductive functions in both women and men.
- **Infertility:** Women who smoke more than 20 cigarettes a day are three times less likely than non-smokers to become pregnant within a year. They also have a greater risk of 'ectopic pregnancy' (a life-threatening condition where the fetus begins to develop in the Fallopian tube instead of in the womb).
- **Menstrual disorders**: pain, pre-menstrual tension, irregularity and amenorrhoea (absence of menstrual periods) are more common in women who smoke.
- The **menopause** tends to be 2–3 years earlier in smokers.
- Women smokers who use **oral contraception** are at greater risk of cardiovascular disease. See p 9.
- Babies born to smoking mothers are on average 0.2 kg lighter – this may be a critical difference that can affect survival. For effects of **maternal smoking on the fetus**, infant and child see Chapter 3.
- Men who smoke produce on average about 24% **fewer sperm**, and have a higher proportion of sperm showing gross defects. There is

increasing evidence that smoking is a major cause of impotence, too, probably from damage to the small blood vessels in the penis (Napier, 1995b).

Fires

Cigarettes (and associated matches and lighters) are a major cause of death and injury from fires and explosions throughout the world. They cause an estimated 900 deaths a year in the US (about 30% of total fire deaths). Worldwide, smoking is estimated to cause 10% of fire deaths a year – about 30,000 people – through burning or suffocation, and about five times that number suffer severe burns and/or inhalation injuries. One in six are children (Leistikow et al., 2000).

Note on the stories about patients with common fatal smoking-related diseases

Most of the patients in the stories included in this chapter had at least some possibility of good medical treatment. In many countries and regions this will not be easily available. Prevention by avoiding smoking is infinitely better than 'cures' which are still uncertain and often not available at all.

General references

Doll R, Crofton J (eds). 1996. Tobacco and health. Br Med Bull 52(1): 1–227.

Doll R, Hill AB. 1950. Smoking and carcinoma of the lung. BMJ ii: 739–748.

Doll R. 1996. Cancers weakly related to smoking. In Doll R, Crofton J (eds). Tobacco and Health. Br Med Bull 52(1): 35–49.

Leistikow BN, Martin DC, Milano CE. 2000. Fire injuries, disasters, and costs from cigarettes and cigarette lighters: A global overview. Preventive Medicine 31: 91.

Liu B-Q, Peto R, Chen Z-M et al. 1998. Emerging tobacco hazards in China: 1. Retrospective proportional mortality study of 1 million deaths. BMJ 317: 1411–1422. 2. Early mortality results from a prospective study. BMJ 317: 1423–1424.

Peto R, Lopez AD et al. 1994. Mortality from smoking in developed countries 1950–2000. Oxford: Oxford University Press.

Peto R, Lopez AD. 2001. Future worldwide health effects of current smoking. In Koop CE, Pearson CE, Schwartz MR. Critical issues in global health. San Francisco: Jossey-Bass. ISBN 0-7879-4824-1.
Simpson D. 2000 Doctors and tobacco. London: Tobacco Control Resource Centre at British Medical Association. ISBN 0-7279-1491-X.
United States Surgeon General. 1982. The health consequences of smoking. USGPO.

References on less familiar topics

ASH Working Group on Women and Smoking. 1995. As Times Goes By. Smoking and the Older Woman. London and Edinburgh: Action on Smoking and Health, Health Education Authority, Health Education Board for Scotland.
Cartwright RA et al. 1983. Cigarette smoking and bladder cancer: an epidemiological inquiry in West Yorkshire. J Epidemiol Community Health 37: 256–263.
Iribarren C et al. 1999. Effect of cigar smoking on the risk of cardiovascular disease, chronic obstructive pulmonary disease, and cancer in men. N Engl J Med 340: 1829–1831.
Kinlen LJ, Rogot E. 1988. Leukaemia and smoking habits among United States veterans. BMJ 297: 657–659.
Mack TM et al. 1986. Pancreas cancer and smoking, beverage consumption, and past medical history. J Natl Cancer Inst 76: 49–60.
Mitchell P, Chapman S, Smith W. 1999. 'Smoking is a major cause of blindness' – A new cigarette pack warning? Med J Austr 171: 173–174.
Napier K. 1995a. Cigarettes: what the warning label doesn't tell you. The first comprehensive guide to the health consequences of smoking. New York: American Council on Science and Health, pp 122–123.
Napier K. 1995b. Cigarettes: what the warning label doesn't tell you. The first comprehensive guide to the health consequences of smoking. New York: American Council on Science and Health, pp 96–100.
Wald NJ, Hackshaw AK. 1996. Cigarette smoking: an epidemiological overview. In Doll R, Crofton J (eds). Tobacco and Health. Br Med Bull 52(1): 7.

3 | Passive Smoking, Second-hand Smoke, Environmental Tobacco Smoke

To non-smokers, tobacco smoke has always been unpleasant. It smells. It chokes. It irritates the nose and eyes. But it is only in the last 20 years or so that research has shown that breathing other people's smoke can also be highly dangerous.

Unborn children are at risk, as well as children whose parents smoke, and adult non-smokers. Although risks are not as great among non-smokers as smokers, a similar range of diseases and disorders results, including cancers, heart disease and stroke, and respiratory conditions such as asthma.

Because of these risks, there have been major efforts in many countries to protect non-smokers from cigarette smoke. Through legislation and persuasion, more and more transport, public places, workplaces and homes are becoming smoke free. This is also helping to create a climate of opinion that motivates smokers to quit.

Ill effects of environmental tobacco smoke (ETS)

On children if parents smoke

Evidence for harm derives chiefly from long-term studies of large numbers of children conceived or born in a certain period (a 'cohort'). In such studies, other relevant factors (income, education, malnutrition etc.) also have to be taken into account in calculating the effect of parental smoking.

These ill effects, which are now clear in a wide range of diseases and disorders, are generally greater if both parents smoke. Of the two parents, it is the mothers' smoke that is usually more damaging.

- **Miscarriage, stillbirth** and **congenital abnormalities** are more common.
- More babies are born **prematurely**, and their **birthweight** tends to be lower. Prematurity and low birthweight both increase the risk of early infant death.

- Cot death (**Sudden Infant Death Syndrome**) is more likely. About 25% of such deaths in apparently healthy infants seem to be associated with mothers' smoking. The risk is nearly doubled if mother smokes 20 or more cigarettes a day (Anderson and Cook, 1997).
- On average, the children of smoking mothers are **smaller** and have lower **academic achievements** both in early and later life.
- Infants under 6 months of age are three times more likely to develop an acute respiratory illness, including pneumonia. In older infants the risk is 50–100% higher. The effect is less definite in older children, who spend more time outside the house.
- **Chronic cough, sputum and wheezing** are twice as common in infants, and 50% higher in children of school age (higher still if they also smoke themselves).
- New cases of **asthma** are 50–100% more common if parents smoke. If a child is an asthmatic, attacks are more frequent and more intense.
- Middle ear disease is more common.
- Young children are at particular risk in closed rooms and confined spaces such as cars, which greatly increase the concentration of dangerous chemicals from second-hand smoke.

Effects of other people's smoke on non-smoking adults

Breathing other people's smoke is not as risky as smoking oneself, but the risks are still significant. Most studies in this area compare the rate of common smoking-related diseases in non-smokers married to smokers with the rate in non-smokers married to non-smokers. Again the risk seems to be 'dose-related' – the more cigarettes the partner smokes, the higher the risk for the non-smoker.

A review of 34 such studies of **lung cancer** showed a combined increased risk of 24% more lung cancer in those exposed to cigarette smoke in the home (Law and Hackshaw, 1996).

There is now mounting evidence of an increased risk of **ischaemic heart disease** (coronary artery disease) of about 25% (Law et al., 1997). A recent study from New Zealand found an even higher excess (82%) for **stroke** (Bonita et al., 1999).

For **chronic respiratory disease** (mainly Chronic Obstructive Pulmonary Disease) some eight studies have shown an excess of 25%. Some, but not all, studies have shown a decrease in **lung function** measurements in those exposed to ETS.

There is less extensive evidence regarding **asthma**, but it does suggest that there is a 40–60% increased risk of developing asthma in adults exposed to ETS at home (Coultas, 1998).

Denying the danger

The tobacco industry is clearly worried that increasing public concern about ETS is affecting their sales. They have created 'smokers' rights' organisations to resist and roll back the tide of clean air legislation, published misleading advertisements claiming the risk of passive smoking is less than for many other activities, and have even hired scientists to 'prove' that ETS may be 'annoying' but it is not harmful.

One criticism the tobacco industry regularly makes of ETS research is that some people studied in the research may have concealed or forgotten that they did indeed once smoke. As smokers tend to marry smokers, there may have been more of these ex-smokers in the supposed 'non-smokers married to smokers' group. If so, this could inflate the numbers of alleged 'non-smokers' falling ill as a result of their partners' smoking.

On the other hand, 'non-smokers' with no exposure to cigarette smoke in the home will almost inevitably have been exposed to it outside the home. This would have increased their risk.

A careful analysis (Wald et al., 1986) concluded that these two possible sources of error cancel each other out. Further studies have confirmed the seriousness of the risks to non-smokers.

Conclusions

- Smoking by mothers risks various damage to the unborn baby, new born baby, infant and child. Some effects last into adult life. Encouraging non-smoking in mothers (while not overdoing the 'guilt' message) must therefore have high priority.
- In adults it is clear that passive smoking increases the risk of lung cancer in non-smokers. There is accumulating evidence that the same is true for ischaemic heart disease, chronic respiratory disease and stroke. Asthma is also more common.
- In many countries, evidence about the harmful effects of passive smoking has had a major effect on public opinion. Demands are growing for smoke-free transport, public places and workplaces (see examples of legislation on pp 105,110). Smoking is becoming more and more socially unacceptable.

General references

Anderson HR, Cook DG. 1997. Passive smoking and sudden infant death syndrome: review of the epidemiological evidence. Thorax 52(11): 1003–1009.

Bonita R, Duncan J, Truelsen T, Jackson RT, Beaglehole R. 1999. Passive smoking as well as active smoking increases the risk of acute stroke. Tobacco Control 8: 156–160.

Coultas DB. 1998. Passive smoking and risk of adult asthma and COPD: an update. Thorax 53: 381–387.

Law MR et al. 1997. Environmental tobacco smoke exposure and ischaemic heart disease: an evaluation of the evidence. BMJ 315: 973–980.

Law MR, Hackshaw AK. 1996. Environmental tobacco smoke. Br Med Bull 52(1): 22–34.

Office of Health and Environmental Assessment. 1992. Respiratory health effects of passive smoking: lung cancer and other disorders. Washington DC: United States Environmental Protection Agency.

Wald NJ, Nanchal K, Thompson SG, Cuckle HS. 1986. Does other people's tobacco smoke cause lung cancer? BMJ 293: 1217–1222.

4 | Smokeless Tobacco (Oral Tobacco)

The WHO has estimated that, worldwide, smokeless tobacco is used by up to 400 million people, causing about 100,000 deaths a year in men and 50,000 in women.

Smokeless tobacco contains more than 2000 chemicals, a number of which may be cancer causing. Just as much nicotine is absorbed as by smoking, though more slowly, so oral tobacco is equally addictive. The health effects are both local in the mouth and general in the body.

Types of use (Table 4.1)

'Dry snuff' (tobacco powder) is inhaled through the nose. Snuff was an extensive habit in Europe and North America in the seventeenth and eighteenth centuries. It is now used mainly by Bantu peoples of South Africa.

In the past, tobacco was often chewed in the form of a roll, plug or twist, especially by sailors and miners. **Chewing tobacco** is associated with cancers of the gum or mouth.

'Moist snuff' of various kinds has a long history of traditional use in certain Asian countries. Most recently it has been produced industrially in the USA and Sweden, where it is provided in small packets like tea bags. The use of these is often termed 'snuff dipping'. The various forms (see Table 4.1) are held in some part of the mouth (between lip and gum, cheek and gum, or under the tongue) for several hours a day.

Betel quid (areca nut with powdered slaked lime and additives wrapped in vine leaf, with or without tobacco) is widely used in South Asian countries. There is good evidence that only the material containing tobacco has a high cancer risk.

In India and Pakistan the use of oral tobacco is widespread in some areas, at all ages, and in women as well as men. It was originally a peasant industry but oral tobacco is now being manufactured and widely advertised by industrial companies. In some countries in Central Asia up to 20% of adults use **'nass'**.

Nasal snuff is widely used by black South Africans and in parts of Asia.

Table 4.1 Smokeless tobacco

Form	Content	Type of use	Area of use
Dry snuff	Powdered tobacco + additives	Inhaled	Bantu of South Africa; formerly N America and Europe
Wet/moist snuff; snuff dipping	Finely cut tobacco in small packets – highly alkaline to encourage nicotine absorption	Held between cheek or lip and gum	USA: 12 million users, mostly young men. Sweden: 20% of all males, increasing use among young women
Chewing tobacco	Tobacco plugs or twists	Chewed	Formerly Southern USA, sailors and miners in Europe
Betel quid	Areca nut + powdered slaked lime + tobacco + additives wrapped in vine leaf	Held between cheek or lip and gum	South Asia
Gutka (see, Gupta, 1999)	Small aluminium foil sachets containing , tobacco, areca nut etc.	Chewed or sucked	India and Bangladesh
Various sweets	Variable amounts of tobacco (often unlabelled)	Chewed or sucked	As above: including children
Gudakhu	Paste of sun-dried tobacco	Cleaning teeth	India: Bihar and Orissa
Kaini	Powdered Indian sun-dried tobacco	Held between cheek and gum	South Asia
Mishri	Sun-dried Indian tobacco heated on a metal plate	Cleaning teeth in women and children; and may be held in the mouth	India

Table 4.1 Smokeless tobacco (*continued*)

Form	Content	Type of use	Area of use
Zarda	Tobacco leaf – boiled with lime and spices, dried, coloured with vegetable dyes	Held in mouth	South Asia
Kiwan	As above, with rose water and spices	Held in mouth	South Asia
Nass	Tobacco, wood ash, oil and usually lime	Held under tongue or between lip and gum	Central Asian republics, parts of Iran, Pakistan, Afghanistan

Ill effects

- **Addiction.** Young users who are addicted to smokeless tobacco may later turn to cigarettes, which are much more lethal. But no one should advocate smokeless tobacco as a 'safer' habit.
- **Leukoplakia** (white patches in the lining of the mouth) is common where the tobacco is usually held. It tends to clear after stopping use of oral tobacco.
- **Gingivitis** etc. (inflammation of gums and around teeth) increases dental caries. The edges of the gums may shrink and the teeth become stained. This does not clear up quickly on quitting oral tobacco use.
- **Oral submucous fibrosis** (scarring in the tissues of the mouth). This fibrosis may lead to contraction (tightening). In extreme cases the patients may only be able to open their mouths to admit a drinking straw. This condition develops rapidly, does not reverse after quitting, and there is no known cure (Gupta, 1999).
- **Oral cancer.** The risk found in different studies has varied, but was as high as four times that in non-users in a US study. In some South-east Asian studies the oral cancer risk in regular users was found to be 10 times higher. Oral cancer is the third commonest cancer in India. Betel quid without tobacco carries a much lower risk.
- **Cardiovascular risks.** Research on cardiovascular risks has given varied results. There may be a slightly increased risk.
- **Nasal snuff.** This may have some ill effects but they have not been well defined. There may be a risk of cancer of the maxillary sinuses.

A brief story about mouth cancer due to oral tobacco
The authors have had little personal experience of this disease. But one of us (JC) is still haunted by a visit to an Indian hospital. In one of the wards of the hospital there was a row of six beds. Each was occupied by a woman with a vast ulcerating cancer mass sprouting out through her cheek. This made him realise what a high priority must be given to preventing these horrors.

Prevention

In recent years US companies have attempted to introduce smokeless tobacco into European and other countries. This was banned by the UK government and subsequently by the European Union (except for Sweden, where there is a long tradition of use). Smokeless tobacco has also been banned in Australia, Israel, Japan, Hong Kong, New Zealand, Saudi Arabia and Singapore.

Efforts are being made in India to reduce the use of smokeless tobacco, but these have to battle with recent advertising campaigns to promote it. One suggestion is to promote switching from betel quid containing tobacco to betel quid without tobacco.

A European law was designed to prevent the introduction of 'Skoal Bandits', a US tobacco product intended to be sucked. However, the law does not ban tobacco designed for chewing, such as sweets containing tobacco. Leaders of Asian communities in the UK are very concerned about the spread of the habit in children. Other countries should be aware of the potential risk both to adults and children.

General references

Gupta PC. 1999. Gutka: a major new tobacco hazard in India. Tobacco Control 8: 134.

Muir CS, Zaridze DG. 1986. Smokeless tobacco and cancer: an overview. In: Zaridze DG, Peto R (eds) Tobacco: a major international health hazard. Lyon: WHO International Agency for Research on Cancer. pp 35–40.

Pershagen G. 1996. Smokeless tobacco. Br Med Bull 52(1): 50–57.

5 Women and Tobacco

In most countries where smoking is a long-standing habit, men were the first to take it up – initially pipes and cigars rather than cigarettes. Even while male rates of smoking increased, it remained fairly unusual among women and was widely thought to be 'improper'. Smoking was often adopted earliest by better-educated and more ambitious women, who regarded it as a sign of sophistication and liberation. Often, women seem to have taken their cue from film stars, for whom cigarettes had become an elegant theatrical prop.

As had already happened with men, deaths from smoking-related diseases duly rose among women, too. Women, particularly better-educated women, went on to quit in great numbers. Nevertheless, in many western countries the habit has now spread so much that smoking rates among young women may even exceed those for young men.

In contrast, in many Asian and African countries smoking rates in women are still low, though in many cases already rising. Most of these countries are at an earlier stage of the smoking epidemic. The contrasts are summarised in Figure 5.1.

The growing world epidemic in women (Figure 5.1)

- **Stage I:** Many low-income countries, especially sub-Saharan Africa. Male smoking rates are often less than 15% but rising rapidly. Female rates are often under 5%. Related deaths are not yet obvious.
- **Stage II:** Latin America, North Africa, and several Asian countries (including China and Japan). Male smoking rates are rising rapidly to 50–80%. There are few ex-smokers. Female rates lag 10–20 years behind, but are increasing. Male deaths are increasing.
- **Stage III:** Eastern and Southern Europe. Male rates are starting to decline to about 40%. Female rates peak at a lower rate than in men. In some countries they are starting to decline, in others they are still rising. Deaths are still rising in men and beginning to rise in women.
- **Stage IV:** USA, UK, Canada, Northern and Western Europe. Smoking rates are slowly declining in both sexes. For example, in the UK,

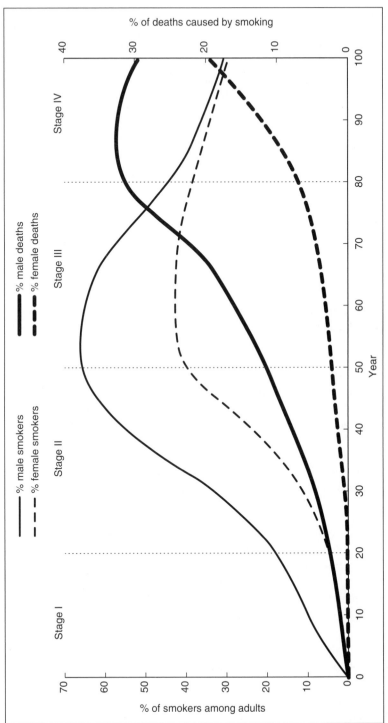

Figure 5.1 A model of the cigarette epidemic. (Adapted from: Amos 1996 Br Med Bull 52(1): 77, with kind permission.)

overall smoking rates among men have fallen from more than 50% in 1974 to 26% in 2000, and among women, from more than 40% to 27% in the same period. However, there is generally much less decline, if any, among the poorest and least skilled. In some countries female rates are overtaking male rates, and male deaths are falling while female deaths are still rising. In a few (e.g. USA, UK), lung cancer has now overtaken breast cancer as the main cause of cancer deaths for women. In many western countries there has also been a worrying recent renewed rise in smoking among young women.

Note that not all countries fit this pattern. For example, female smoking rates are exceptionally high in some low-income countries, including Nepal, Papua New Guinea, Northern Thailand, and some areas of India. They are also very high among Maori women in New Zealand.

Why Are Women Special?

- In many countries, women's smoking rates are much lower than men's. Increased independence and earning-power make women a vast potential market, especially in the expanding economies of Asia.
- Tobacco companies are well aware of this, and seek to make smoking smart, fashionable and 'Western' – a sign of affluence, social ease, and sophistication. On the other hand, cigarettes are also associated with helping women cope with some of the *problems* of modernity, including stress and the need to be sexually attractive.
- Where the spread of smoking is recent among women, smoking-related deaths are low. Women (and even women's organisations and public health doctors) may not fully realise the threat to women's health, and to the health of their children.
- Reasons for women and girls starting to smoke, and the difficulties they may face in stopping, may be different from men's. Health promotion experts have often been slow to realise that women may need a very different approach from men.
- Some obstacles in quitting are more important among women, e.g. fears of weight gain, and feelings of social dependence. Many women describe smoking as their 'only luxury'.

Health risks of tobacco in women

It is estimated that between 1950 and 2000, 10 million women in the world died from smoking-related diseases.

The main health risks to women are no different from those for men. As Professor Sir Richard Peto of the University of Oxford, UK has written, 'If women smoke like men, they will die like men'.

For the health risks women smokers share with men, and for the risks associated with female reproduction, see Chapter 2. Smoking mothers also risk damage to their children, both before and after birth (see Chapter 3). In some countries, notably in South Asia, smokeless tobacco causes much death and illness in women (see Chapter 4). In India, some women use an unusual method of smoking with the burning end inside the mouth. This results in high levels of mouth cancer.

In poor countries, women may particularly suffer from the husband's smoking through exposure to Environmental Tobacco Smoke (see Chapter 3). This may be made worse by exposure to smoke from cooking or heating fires in houses without chimneys. In addition, more of a tiny family income may be spent on tobacco, which itself threatens family health.

Cosmetic damage

In addition to threatening life, research has shown that cigarette smoke is an important cause of premature wrinkles and, possibly, grey hair. Together with bad breath and stained teeth and fingernails, this may be worth emphasising in health education directed at women.

Figure 5.2

Targeting by tobacco companies

In western countries, the increase in smoking among women is associated with the development of 'feminised' cigarettes – filter tips to reduce tar staining, milder, less pungent tobaccos, and cigarettes made longer and thinner. Menthol and so-called 'light' or 'low tar' brands were introduced to calm health fears. Packaging was redesigned to imply elegance and slimness. Throughout the world, this 'feminising' of the cigarette continues to help overcome taboos against women smoking.

Cigarettes are widely advertised and featured in many media, including women's magazines, where they are associated with social success, self-confidence, reducing stress, calming 'nerves', and controlling body weight – all of which are intended to appeal to adolescents and young women. Magazines and newspapers that carry tobacco advertising may have fewer articles about tobacco and health.

Tobacco companies target women through sponsoring popular music, discos, television, films, video and sports with a high female appeal. For example, they promote fashion events, where models are seen and photographed smoking. Similarly, female sports stars have been recruited to endorse brands, or use branded sportswear.

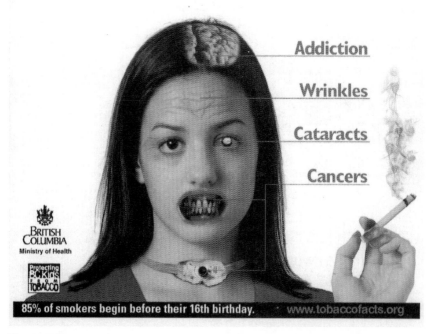

Figure 5.3

Figure 5.4

In countries with low rates of women smoking, advertising and other forms of promotion typically seek to represent smoking as modern, attractive, fashionable and 'Western'.

Poverty and smoking

This is mainly a problem for western countries in the later stages of a smoking epidemic (Stage IV, Figure 5.1). In these countries smoking rates are usually much higher in poorer households and in poorer areas (ASH, 1993). In better-off households more adults have quit and fewer children have started smoking. In Britain, for example, smoking rates in households of unskilled workers are double those in professional households. Among women who are unemployed, divorced, separated or single mothers, the rates are higher still.

Reasons why poor women smoke

Poor women in industrialised countries may not *fully* understand the risks to health, but they do usually know that smoking is very harmful to themselves and their children. (Elsewhere, poor women may not know the risks at all.) Furthermore, cigarettes are expensive, and take money away from already-stretched budgets. So why does smoking remain 'normal' among poor women – one of the 'necessities of life'?

It would be a mistake to imply that such women do not care about their health and the health of their families. On the contrary, they may care very much indeed. Part of the answer could lie in a belief that the *benefits* of smoking outweigh the harm it does, at least in the short term. In this view, cigarettes can almost seem like a form of self-medication.

Poor women with young children can be very lonely, and suffer much financial and other stress, particularly if they are confined to the home and have no supporting relatives. Cigarettes may be their only answer to stress. When today and tomorrow look so hopeless, possible ill-health in the remote future has much less meaning. Such women describe cigarettes as 'my only luxury … the only thing I do for myself'. They 'make me less irritable with the children' … 'a short break with a smoke helps me to cope'. In short, they often believe it makes them better rather than worse mothers.

Possible remedies

For all these reasons few countries have yet been very successful in reducing smoking in poor households. In the longer term, reducing poverty and improving education will, let us hope, gradually reduce smoking. But what can be done now?

Substitutes for relieving stress could be useful, for example:

- Community development projects that encourage local groups to be actively involved with their health and to share experiences and problems. Group support for quitting has been successful in western countries among patients addicted to tranquillisers. The same could be true for smoking. Pamphlets on quitting are more likely to be fully understood if they are rewritten by local women in their own language.
- 'Alternative' medicines and therapies have particular appeal if they are administered by a sympathetic person who listens to the woman's problems. Examples are acupuncture, hypnotherapy and homeopathy. Research evidence is lacking, but these therapies may be helpful in women with anxiety or mild depression, which often underlie their addiction to cigarettes.
- Formal counselling groups may provide both advice and support.
- For those in work, making more and more workplaces smoke free will help.

There is still much room for research to find better ways of helping.

Taxation, smoking and poverty

Raising tobacco tax reduces consumption (p100) but also increases poverty in continuing smokers. This is a dilemma for policy makers. The World Bank recommends providing free or subsidised nicotine substitutes as a cost-effective means of helping the poor become less poor by quitting (World Bank, 1999).

Figure 5.5

Prevention

Countries with low or rising smoking rates in women must organise immediately to prevent the spread of the tobacco epidemic. Efforts must be made to:
- Involve women in all national and local Tobacco Control Programmes and in planning health education programmes.
- Influence women's groups, associations and societies.

- Influence health professionals, including doctors (e.g. GPs, obstetricians, paediatricians, midwives, and nurses) to pay special attention to women smokers. Antenatal education should include quitting help both for the sake of the infant and the mother. Health workers should encourage mothers to quit permanently, not just during pregnancy.
- Encourage health education through popular media, e.g. the incorporation of quit-smoking storylines in 'soap operas' on radio or television.

General references

Amos A. 1996. Women and smoking. Br Med Bull 52(1): 74–89.

ASH Scotland/Health Education Board for Scotland. 1999. Women. Low income and smoking. Breaking down the barriers. Edinburgh: ASH, HEBS.
Describes various community development approaches to helping smokers to stop and building up non-smoking habits in multi-deprived areas in Scotland. Available from Action on Smoking and Health Scotland (ASH), 8 Frederick Street, Edinburgh EH2 2HB, Scotland.

ASH Working Group on Women and Smoking. 1993. Her share of misfortune. Women, smoking and low income. London: Action on Smoking and Health. ISBN 1-872428-05-3.

Chollat-Traquet C. 1992. Women and tobacco. Geneva: World Health Organization.

Simpson D. 2000. Doctors and tobacco. London: Tobacco Control Resource Centre at British Medical Association. pp 11–12. ISBN 0-7279-1491-X

World Bank. 1999. Curbing the epidemic. Governments and the economics of tobacco control. Washington: The World Bank. ISBN 0-8213-4519-2.

6 | Children and Adolescents

Health effects of tobacco smoke on children

When parents smoke

We have outlined the direct health effects of parents' smoking on the fetus, and on children, in Chapter 3. These ill effects, which are clear in a wide range of diseases and disorders, are generally greater if both parents smoke. Of the two parents, it is the mother's smoke that is usually more damaging.

But the damage does not stop there. The children of parents who smoke are more likely to become smokers themselves. Later, as parents, they repeat the pattern.

Most of the evidence comes from western countries, but health risks may prove even worse in lower-income countries where cigarettes may have a higher tar content, and where living space is smaller or more crowded. Here, children are even more exposed to the dense smoke from adults' cigarettes.

When children smoke

Regular cigarette use, starting in teenage years, gives you a 50:50 chance of dying prematurely from a smoking-related disease. Young smokers who give up avoid virtually all of these risks.

The earlier children start smoking, the more likely they are to continue smoking throughout life, to smoke heavily, and to die from a smoking-related disease. The younger they take up smoking, on average the younger they are when they suffer from heart attacks or lung cancer.

> **Early health damage**
> Damage does not only occur in the longer term. Compared with non-smoking children, children who smoke even a few cigarettes a week:
> - suffer more frequent colds and coughs,
> - have more frequent ear infections,

- miss more school due to illness,
- have more hospital admissions,
- are six times more likely to suffer a subarachnoid brain haemorrhage.

Children who smoke are also less fit athletically – they are slower both at sprints and endurance running. This is partly an effect of lung function (Royal College of Physicians of London, 1992). In all people, the efficiency of the lungs declines with age, but the lungs of children who smoke 'age' much faster than those of their non-smoking peers. For example, a 16-year-old who smokes 20 cigarettes a day might in effect have the lungs of a 28-year-old non-smoker.

Why children start smoking

It takes remarkably few cigarettes to 'hook' a child. For some, no more than 5 cigarettes, or 4 weeks' occasional use, are enough to produce classic symptoms of nicotine dependence – cravings, depressed mood, irritability, frustration, anxiety, difficulty concentrating, and restlessness. Children as young as 11 years old report withdrawal symptoms during periods of abstinence, and loss of control over the amount or duration of use (DiFranza et al., 2000).

Home

If their parents smoke, children tend to do so as well. Clearly, it is easier for children to get hold of cigarettes in a smoking family. They also get used to the smell and irritating effects of smoke, which might otherwise have put them off, at least for a few more years. Some parents even give their children cigarettes to smoke from a very young age.

Naturally, children tend to copy their parents, and older brothers or sisters. (Indeed, a number of studies have shown smoking brothers and sisters have an even bigger influence than smoking parents.) But strong disapproval from parents (even smoking parents) has often been shown to discourage smoking in their children (Royal College of Physicians of London, 1992). Conversely, ex-smokers often cite the influence of their children in prompting them to stop.

School and peer group

In most western countries, efforts are made to educate children before they get to the age when many start to smoke. Almost all children in primary schools (i.e. aged between 5 and 11 years) are strongly opposed

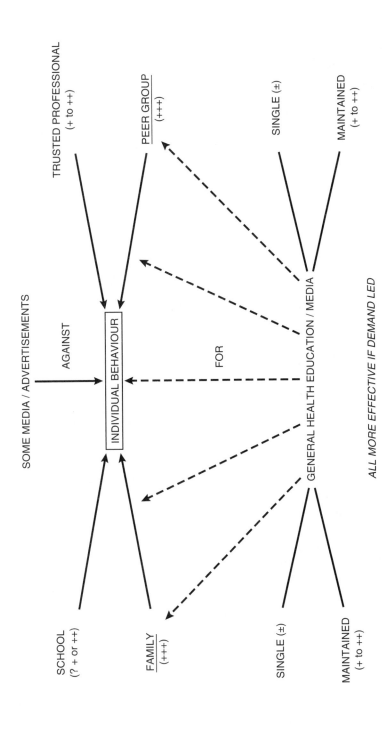

Figure 6.1 Factors affecting individual health behaviour. The number of +++s indicates our assessment of the strength of the effect.

to smoking. But when they move on to 'big school', around age 12 or 13, peer pressure and other influences become increasingly irresistible. If friends and older children at school smoke, the younger child is more likely to join in.

At first it may be part of the social 'get-together'. Children tend to smoke in groups, perhaps pooling money and sharing cigarettes. Often, they don't smoke at all when alone. Smoking rates are also typically lower during school holidays, when peer pressures may weaken, but rates climb again as soon as children return to school. This also suggests smoking may be used, even by young teens, to manage tension, increase self-confidence, and boost self-esteem.

It is not only 'under-achievers' in schoolwork or sport who take up smoking. It may also be common among 'high status' – able, attractive, popular – young people (particularly girls), where it is widely seen as a mark of being 'cool'.

Of course, smoking is a well-known form of risk-taking and a symbol of rebelliousness against adult authority – a fact the tobacco industry has appreciated for a very long time. According to Philip Morris:

> A cigarette for the beginner is a symbolic act. 'I am no longer my mother's child', 'I'm tough', 'I am an adventurer', 'I'm not square'. As the force from the psychological symbolism subsides, the pharmacological effect takes over to sustain the habit.
>
> Philip Morris, Vice President for Research and Development,
> Why one smokes, 1969. Minnesota Trial Exhibit 3681

There is some evidence that smoking is also associated with other forms of risk-taking, such as early sexual intercourse, and the abuse of alcohol and drugs. Some researchers think tobacco may even be an important 'gateway drug' paving the way to e.g. the smoking of cannabis. (The reverse may also be true.)

Adolescents often say they will easily quit later. They greatly underestimate the risks of smoking, the likelihood of long-term tobacco addiction, and the eventual difficulty of stopping.

Worryingly, many teenagers turn the anti-smoking health message that it is 'never too late to stop' into an argument for continuing to smoke – that any damage done in the present can be repaired later, 'when I'm 30'.

This is not to say that school policy can have no influence on smoking. On the contrary – to children, teachers are figures of authority. If the teacher smokes, smoking must be an OK adult activity. Conversely, there is evidence that when teachers are not allowed to smoke in school, smoking rates in children are lower than in schools where teachers are allowed to smoke.

The influence of wider culture

Children naturally have, or seek, adult role models – people they look up to, and try to copy. At first these may be parents. Later they are likely to be sporting figures, or racing car drivers, pop stars, film and TV actors, fashion models. These adult role models vary with country, community, and of course with the age of the child. They may even be largely mythical characters, like the American cowboy in Marlboro cigarette advertisements. If the heroes or heroines appear to smoke, children are more likely to copy them.

The tobacco industry knows this and exploits it ruthlessly. On the other hand, non-smoking popular role models can be very useful allies for health promotion to children.

The tobacco industry and children

Most research on the tobacco industry and children has been done in western countries with a long history of smoking. The results can be of great value to countries at an earlier stage of the tobacco epidemic.

The industry must recruit large numbers of new smokers to replace those who have died, plus others who successfully quit the habit. Since almost all adult smokers start in childhood or adolescence, and smokers are less likely to become addicted if they start later, children and adolescents are the industry's prime targets.

Of course the tobacco companies deny that they target this group. But internal industry documents brought to light in US litigation cases have confirmed that children are indeed central to the industry's commercial success.

The tobacco industry often claims that it is against under-age smoking. It has even begun to fund extensive child-education campaigns, claiming it is acting in a socially responsible way. Their campaigns are no such thing. Publications typically have the corporation's name and colours prominently displayed, sometimes with a Government health warning. And the central message is always the same: 'Smoking is an adult activity. Wait till you are grown-up.' Can you imagine a more persuasive argument to get children to smoke?

There is evidence that tobacco companies have even engineered their cigarettes to make them both more addictive and more palatable to children. For example, from the 1970s many companies added sweeteners to tobacco, such as cocoa, liquorice root, syrup, caramel and dried fruits.

Figure 6.2 (TOLES © The Buffalo News. Reprinted with permission of UNIVERSAL PRESS SYNDICATE. All rights reserved)

Advertising

In many western countries, advertisements for cigarettes are – or soon will be – banned or restricted on television, radio, street hoardings and in newspapers and magazines, particularly those targeted at the young. And there are very good reasons for these bans. Much research has shown that even very young children are familiar with widely advertised cigarette brand names. They have a quite remarkable awareness of advertisements, and an ability to recall them in detail after only one or two viewings – indeed, far more awareness than adults. In consequence, the brands smoked by young people are typically not those most widely smoked by adults, but the ones that are most-prominently advertised. This is particularly true of imported US brands, which often have a particular cachet with the style-conscious young.

Tobacco advertising to children aims to create an atmosphere around smoking and cigarette brands that will attract children. It associates smoking with children's role models and with success, fun, glamour, vitality and freedom.

TELL ME ... DO YOU THINK THE TOBACCO COMPANIES ARE
REALLY TARGETING KIDS ?...

Figure 6.3 (Reproduced with kind permission of Tribune Media Services, Chicago)

But even where advertising is banned in young people's media, children see cigarette brand images in many places. In many countries, some women's magazines, including those largely read by adolescents, contain tobacco advertisements. Even where there are no adverts for cigarettes, fashion models and pop stars are depicted smoking. The way such people use cigarettes is itself a 'style statement'. Such magazines have few or no articles on the dangers of smoking – tobacco companies threaten to remove advertisements if they publish such articles. (For further details see Chapter 9 on the Tobacco Industry.)

Direct promotion and sponsorship of events

In many countries, free sample cigarettes are given out to young people, or full packs exchanged for empty packs of another brand. This may occur in places where young people normally gather, such as bars and clubs, or at specially arranged, prominently advertised events, including pop concerts, discos and dance competitions.

An example of direct promotion
A French tobacco company recruited attractive young women, provided them with fashionable expensive clothing, and paid them to smoke the company's product and give away free samples in clubs.

Sports sponsorship in particular has an immense appeal to young people. Commercially it is most successful if the sport is shown on television nationally or, even better, internationally. An example is Formula 1 motor car racing.

The ease with which satellite broadcasts from abroad can get round national restrictions on tobacco-promotion is clearly something to be concerned about.

'Product placement'

Tobacco companies have paid to have their brands very obviously shown and smoked in films (movies) popular with children. Many are also distributed widely as videos, and hence viewed more frequently.

They have also paid well-known athletes to smoke their brand (or in the USA to use 'moist snuff'), or to use sportswear with the colours or logo of that brand.

'Brand stretching'

Indirect advertising, for example 'brand stretching', becomes increasingly important in countries where direct advertising is banned. Brand stretching means to sell, or license third parties to sell, products other than cigarettes with cigarette brand names or colours. Sometimes these goods are related to smoking, such as cigarette lighters. Increasingly, they are not. Examples include fashionable clothing, shoes, and bags targeted chiefly at young people. Many such items play on an association with adventure or outdoor life, for example Camel boots or Marlboro adventure holidays. Research shows that children assume that these are advertisements for cigarettes.

Candy (sweet) cigarettes

In the past there has been collusion between tobacco and confectionery manufacturers to produce 'candy cigarettes' for children. Packets were often made to resemble those of cigarette brands. There is evidence that this encouraged the young to smoke. With the development of public concern, especially in the USA, such collusion has stopped there, at least formally. A number of countries (including Australia, Finland. Norway, UK, and several Arab countries) have banned confectionery resembling cigarettes (Klein and St Clair, 2000).

Figure 6.4 (Reproduced with kind permission of Creators Syndicate)

Preventing smoking in children

The main aims in preventing smoking-related diseases are to stop children becoming smokers and to help adult smokers to quit. So it is all too easy to say 'we must start with the children'. True, we have to devise programmes targeted at the young. But we should not overestimate the likely benefits, especially in the short term. Nor should we underestimate the difficulties, especially where other influences encourage young people to start. So far we have been far more successful in persuading adults to quit smoking than in persuading children not to start. The best results to date have been where programmes targeted at young people are part of a systematic effort aimed at the whole community (Charlton and Moyer, 1991).

Family and home

Persuading parents – both mothers and fathers – to quit will help to break the damaging 'family circle' that reproduces patterns of smoking and ill-health generation after generation.

Health workers and others can explain to future parents the importance of giving up smoking well before they try to conceive. Helping pregnant women and their partners to quit should be part of antenatal care (p 42). Postnatal care should help young parents who quit during pregnancy not to return to smoking after the birth.

It is important to emphasise parental example, and of parents' attitudes (even when parents themselves continue to smoke). Campaigns can be mounted to persuade parents and other adults not to smoke around children, particularly in confined spaces such as cars.

Schools

Many school programmes aimed at stopping children from smoking have proved unsuccessful in the long term. Young people are notoriously immune to knowledge of the diseases they could contract, and have little understanding of the idea of 'risk'. They find it hard to identify with people of (as they see it) great age.

Some major school education programmes have performed well in early trials, but their effectiveness seems to have dropped off rapidly after the experiment finished (partly because of lack of funds, poor ongoing training, and waning interest).

Yet there is good evidence that schools can make a difference, if only in delaying the age of taking up smoking. Making schools completely 'smoke free' has an effect. In such a school neither teachers nor pupils are allowed to smoke on school premises. There is much still to be learnt in this field. Look out for future developments.

Obviously success is more difficult in an area where there is a high smoking rate among adults. But remember that children often greatly overestimate the number of adults who smoke. They may believe that smoking is normal even when smokers are only a minority.

But we should not despair. Education campaigns may not persuade all young people not to start. Yet in some countries smoking is at a much lower level than 20 years ago, and even most addicted young smokers say they expect to give up in the foreseeable future.

There seems no substitute for a constant supply of well-organised, well-resourced education. Education mainly aims to teach basic knowledge of the health effects of smoking and to develop the personal social skills to resist social and marketing pressures to smoke.

For younger children (7–11 years), it may be useful to involve parents to reinforce the message in the home. But with teens, experience in western countries is that it is better not to involve parents directly.

Bringing a doctor or other expert into the classroom from outside is neither necessary nor particularly effective. Knowledge can be taught (together with the problems of alcohol and drugs, if these are important in that society) by properly trained school staff, including school nurses, within the school curriculum, and from an early age (e.g. 7–11 years).

Knowledge of 'the facts' alone does not alter behaviour. Discussion is important, and the development of skills to analyse and resist social and tobacco industry pressures. Role play and rehearsal of strategies to cope with possible future encounters are often useful. Such work may also be more effective if one or two older children help lead discussions or act as 'peer counsellors'.

Many health educationalists are opposed to using 'shock–horror' tactics, such as showing children actual diseased organs or explicit medical photographs. On the other hand, many young people say this would indeed influence them.

There is more evidence to support educating young people about the activities of the tobacco industry itself. Teens readily understand how they are being cynically exploited.

By their mid-teens, many child smokers want to quit, but find they have become addicted to cigarettes. Therefore, they may need the same sort of help as adults. But so far methods have proved less successful than in adults, partly because of the rather chaotic patterns of adolescent smoking.

Children's organisations

Ideally, all youth clubs and groups should be smoke free. In practice, this may be difficult because many youth workers smoke (even using the offer of cigarettes to promote conversation), and fear that they could be excluding the very 'hard-to-reach' young people they want to attract.

Every effort should be made to educate adults in how they can help the young people they work with.

Smoke-free public places

These are as important for children as they are for adults. As they increase in number and scale, children will find there are fewer places they can smoke, and increasingly feel that non-smoking is the normal thing for adults.

Health professionals

Doctors, nurses and other health professionals should repeatedly advocate non-smoking in their contacts with families and children (Chapter 8, p 76). Of course they should also set a good example by not smoking themselves, and try to make their clinics, health centres and hospitals smoke free.

Tobacco advertising

Banning of all forms of advertising and promotion, including sponsorship, whether targeted at children or at adults, should be a major part of any national programme (Chapter 10). Fortunately, more and more governments are doing this. Also the international governing bodies of some sports, including football, have outlawed tobacco promotion.

Sales of cigarettes to children

(In most countries, 'children' are defined as those aged under 16. In some US states this has been raised to 18.)

It is very hard to ban children from smoking. Laws that prohibit 'under-age sales' of cigarettes are more common, and are well worthwhile, but can be difficult to enforce. Trading standards officials may be too few, or too reluctant, to act effectively; many countries are opposed to identity or 'proof of age' cards, and some courts will not allow evidence if underage children are used as decoys to catch rogue traders. Success in halting sales calls for adequate funding, tight co-ordination and monitoring, and heavy penalties.

Tobacco companies often back such laws, which suggests they are ineffective. The laws may even add to the 'forbidden fruit' attraction of cigarettes. But at least such a law indicates government disapproval. (See also Chapter 10, p 108.)

Price

The price of cigarettes has a powerful effect on smoking prevention and cessation rates. Low prices (including low taxes) encourage smoking. Repeated price rises cut overall consumption and increase the numbers of adults who quit (p 100). There is good evidence that they have an even bigger impact on children and adolescents (Figure 6.5).

Mass media campaigns

Unless free broadcasting time is available, mass media campaigns are very expensive to mount and maintain.

Most campaigns are directed at adults, not young people. Even so, there is some evidence that they can influence children directly. They certainly reveal a pool of need. A television campaign in Scotland that promoted a free telephone 'Quit-line' was surprised by the number of calls from children. (It is not clear how many children succeeded in quitting as a result because they were reluctant to give their telephone numbers to researchers for follow-up study.)

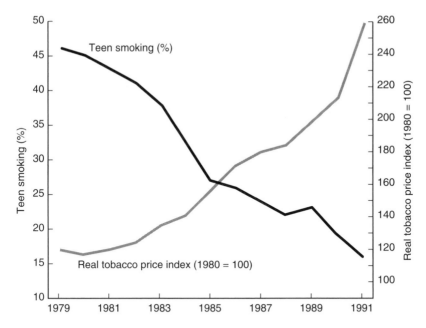

Figure 6.5 Real cigarette prices and cigarette smoking among Canadians age 15–19. (Adapted from: American Cancer Society: World Smoking and Health. Children and Tobacco. 1992; 17(3):10, with kind permission.)

The appeals that seem most persuasive to young people are those that focus on the actions of the tobacco industry, not on the teen's immediate or long-term personal health. Some of the most successful youth-oriented campaigns have a significant creative input from teens.

Persuading children not to start smoking is one of the major challenges in tobacco control. But it is no use concentrating on children alone. There will be much greater success if the efforts for children are part of a comprehensive tobacco control policy. There are seldom dramatic effects. But now in many countries smoking has substantially, if slowly, decreased both for adults and for children.

General references

Bailey D, Hawes H, Monati G. 1994. Child-to-Child: a resource book. Part 2. The Child-to-Child activity sheets. 2nd edn. London: Child-to-Child Trust.

Obtainable from TALC, UK (see Appendix B). Activity Sheet 7.1. Smoking – think for yourself. pp 133–136. Designed for 10–14-year-olds. Produced in association with Save the Children and CAFOD. It has been increasingly used in Asian, African, and Latin American schools.

Charlton A, Moyer C (eds). 1991. Children and tobacco: the wider view. Geneva: International Union against Cancer. ISBN 2-88236-003-7. An earlier, more global review.

Charlton A. 1996. Children and smoking: the family circle. In Doll R, Crofton J. Br Med Bull 52(1): 90–107.
A briefer review largely concerned with industrialised countries.

DiFranza JR, Rigotti NA, McNeill AD, Ockene JK, Savageau JA, St Cyr D, Coleman M. 2000. Initial symptoms of nicotine dependence in adolescents. Tobacco Control 9: 313–319.

Hawes H (ed.). 1997. Health promotion in our schools. Child-to-Child Trust/UNICEF. ISBN 0-946182-10-8.
Obtainable from TALC, UK (see Appendix B). A very practical book on the subject. It is primarily designed for tropical countries. It could be very helpful as a guide in starting health promotion in schools. The tobacco problem could be easily included in such a programme. Much emphasis on children and educators.

Klein JD, St Clair S. 2000. Do candy cigarettes encourage young people to smoke? BMJ 321: 362–365.

Royal College of Physicians of London. 1992. Smoking and the young. London: Royal College of Physicians. ISBN 1-873240-42-2.

World Bank. 1999. Curbing the epidemic. Governments and the economics of tobacco control. Washington: World Bank. ISBN 0-8213-4519-2.
Although basically concerned with economics and government actions, contains many useful and up-to-date conclusions from recent resarch, including research on children's smoking.

US Department of Health and Human Services. 1994. Preventing tobacco use among young people. A report by the Surgeon General. Atlanta, Georgia: US Department of Health and Human Services, Public Health Service, Centers for Disease Control and Prevention, National Center for Chronic Disease Prevention and Health Promotion, Office on Smoking and Health.
Particularly concerned with USA.

7 Quitting

The main reasons why people want to stop smoking are obvious: concerns about health – their own, their family's and that of anyone who breathes their smoke – and money. Many people also recognise that smoking is a deeply unpleasant habit. It is smelly and dirty, and encourages young people to take up an unhealthy habit. Some people are also motivated by worries about environmental damage; or by concerns about tobacco crops occupying land that could otherwise be used to grow food crops. Increasingly, people are appalled by the reckless behaviour of multinational tobacco companies.

The profoundly harmful effects of smoking are now well established, but not universally known. A smoker's knowledge of the facts about these harmful effects varies between and within countries, and is partly related to the level of education but mainly to the extent of public health campaigns. In some countries many smokers have very little idea of the true risks of smoking.

The financial effects should be self-evident (though in fact many smokers are amazed when they calculate the total they are spending every month). Over a lifetime, smokers pay tobacco companies (and governments, in the form of taxes) vast sums of money for no obvious benefit.

Mr Wong, aged 30, worked as a clerk in an office. He started smoking when he was 17. He smoked 15 cigarettes a day. In his 20s he began to have a smoker's cough. (This was probably the early stages of Chronic Obstructive Pulmonary Disease: see Chapter 2.) He had two young children. His wife did not smoke, and was always trying to persuade him to quit. He said he would do so 'sometime' – but he kept on putting it off. The cough got worse. He tried to stop several times. But each time, the craving got too much for him and he was back smoking again within a week.

One winter he developed a bad cold that went to his chest. He became feverish. He went to see a doctor who diagnosed 'a touch of pneumonia'. The doctor asked him about his smoking and strongly advised Mr Wong to quit. He warned him that if he didn't, his chest would gradually worsen. He told Mrs Wong the same. Mr and Mrs Wong agreed that she would throw away his cigarettes. Each week he would put the amount of money he would have spent on cigarettes into a special jar.

The doctor gave Mr Wong an antibiotic. He saw him again a week later. His cough was better. His fever had gone. The doctor praised him for having quit smoking and encouraged him to keep it up. His wife was delighted.

With his wife's support Mr Wong kept off cigarettes. He found his wife's cooking much tastier. His cough gradually disappeared. After a few months they were able to have a holiday on the money he had saved.

So why is education about smoking not enough? Why don't all smokers stop as soon as they are told 'the facts'?

There are two main answers: physical addiction to nicotine, and the habituation that means smoking becomes a social and psychological prop. Once a smoker is hooked, stopping can be difficult and unpleasant. To help someone to stop smoking it is wise to consider how easy or difficult this could be for them. This depends largely on two factors:
1. How strong is the motivation to stop?
2. How strong is the addiction?

It is important to think about both factors because they will help you to decide what type of support best suits that smoker. This applies whether you are a doctor trying to help an individual patient, a public health worker planning how to help a large number of smokers in the community, or just someone trying to help a friend or a relative. Light

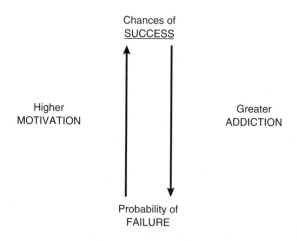

Figure 7.1 Quitting.

smokers eager to stop may need only brief and simple methods. But highly addicted, seriously discouraged heavy smokers may be much more difficult to help.

Motivation

Many people want to stop smoking but, because of addiction, find it difficult to do so. Often it takes several attempts before they succeed. Nevertheless very many do finally succeed – as shown by the great increase in numbers of ex-smokers in many countries. The high failure rate at first attempts to quit can be depressing both to smokers and those trying to help them stop. But the fact that they have tried indicates that they have some degree of motivation and that they may well succeed in the end – and they often do.

Measuring motivation

One simple way is to put a 'multiple choice question' as follows (with suggested scoring):

How much do you want to stop smoking completely?

Not at all (0)
Slightly (1)
Moderately (2)
Quite strongly (3)
Very strongly (4)

Addiction

There are two basic aspects of addiction:

Physical addiction

Physical or chemical addiction is due to the nicotine in the tobacco. Nicotine, like other drugs such as morphine or heroin, provides some pleasant effects. But as with these other addictive drugs, when nicotine is not regularly and instantly available, the smoker gets various unpleasant cravings. The intensity and frequency of nicotine craving mean that all too often the recent ex-smoker returns to smoking after a few days.

Measuring the severity of addiction

In general the more cigarettes smoked per day, the greater the addiction. And if the first cigarette is always smoked within half an hour of waking, addiction is probably severe. These are obvious rules of thumb, but the more elaborate Fagerstrom Index can give a more precise measure (see Appendix 7.1 on page 71).

Some people experience withdrawal symptoms after quitting. These can range from restlessness, irritability and difficulty in concentrating, to anxiety, insomnia and depression. They may also find their appetite increases (which some may welcome) and that they gain weight (which may be unwelcome).

Until recently, there was no way for recent ex-smokers to be given the nicotine without the tobacco. Nicotine replacement therapies (NRT) are now able to do this quite successfully, which can significantly increase the likelihood of long-term success (see below).

But breaking the physical addiction to nicotine may be only a part of the problem. Some people may give up for weeks, months or even years, only to relapse later. They can cope perfectly well with physical cravings and other side effects of nicotine withdrawal. But they cannot break with the social or psychological 'support' provided by smoking.

Social/psychological dependence

Smoking becomes powerfully linked to specific activities. For example some people smoke whenever they take a break with a cup of tea or coffee, or with an alcoholic drink in the evening, or after a meal. Smokers also often believe cigarettes relax them – they say smoking helps with depression or relieves stress, gives them a sense of control, or promotes confidence when meeting strangers. For some, smoking 'fills the time when you're bored' or is simply 'something to do with your hands'.

Stages of change
Many people who design cessation services or who counsel smokers use the 'Stage of Change' model of behaviour.
- **Pre-contemplation.** The smoker has not even considered quitting. Here you can only begin to introduce the idea. You may have to come back to the subject again later.
- **Contemplation.** The smoker begins to think about quitting. This stage may be reached for any number of reasons, including:
  - the advice of a health worker
  - because of what the smoker learns from the media or from friends or family
  - because of illness or some symptom thought by the smoker to be the beginning of a smoking-related illness

- because she has become pregnant or has learnt of the dangers to children.
- **Readiness.** The smoker has now begun to think it is time they ought to quit. But they may well have no confidence that they will succeed. You can help to build up their confidence so that at least they are prepared to have a try. Emphasise the advantages to health and in saving money. Don't rush them. Come back to it each time you see them.
- **Action.** When they are really prepared to have a go, various events in their lives may trigger this final action phase.

Action by health professionals

Doctors are in a good position to help because:
- They are trusted on health matters.
- They see people when they are more likely to accept health advice.
- They can advise in the light of each patient's health problems.
- They see many smoking patients every week.

More information can be found in Richmond, 1994; Fiore et al., 1996; Foulds, 1996; Raw et al., 1998 and Simpson, 2000.

What the doctor should do

- Ask all patients whether they smoke.
- Mark the notes of smokers so that the subject can be raised again.
- Raise the possibility of quitting with all smokers. Do so particularly if symptoms may be related to smoking.
- Be sympathetic and helpful, not challenging or aggressive.
- If the patient does not wish to consider quitting, note this and raise the matter again at later interviews.
- It the patient might consider quitting, give preliminary counselling, and perhaps a pamphlet if available, and arrange to see again.
- If the patient does seem really motivated and is a light or moderate smoker:
- consider asking the patient to fill in a questionnaire about his/her smoking habits;
- suggest they fix a date for quitting;
- suggest temporarily avoiding routine occasions associated with smoking;
- suggest substituting other routines;
- arrange a follow-up appointment about a week after the quit-date. (The expectation of follow-up meetings or phone calls help to prevent relapse.)

- If the patient is a heavy smoker and obviously addicted, prescribe a nicotine substitute if available and if the patient can afford it (p 63).
- The very addicted may need additional counselling, follow-up and group support. Refer to a special clinic (p 66) if available.

Weight gain

The possibility of weight gain can be a particular worry, especially for women. In fact, weight gain is neither inevitable nor likely to be great. It is usually less while on nicotine substitutes. It is best to advise the patient not to try to deal with the weight gain until he or she has got over the early withdrawal symptoms. Then give the usual advice on diet and exercise.

There is no magic cure

The doctor must make it clear that the effort must come from the patient. The doctor can help with advice and support, and may be able to help by prescribing a nicotine substitute.

Dealing with 'failure'

Many people find it difficult to quit smoking, and it often takes several attempts before they succeed. The high failure rate at first attempts to quit can be depressing both to smokers and those trying to help them stop. But the fact that they have tried to stop is a sign that they may well succeed in the end. In the words of a recent campaign, 'Don't give up giving up'.

Mrs Hara started smoking at the age of 14. Ten years later, when she met her future husband, she was smoking 30 cigarettes a day. She had tried to quit a couple of times but failed. Then her father had a stroke. This stimulated her to try again. Her future husband decided to try too. They had a fun bet with each other for a moderate sum. The first one to crack had to pay up. Neither cracked. The money saved helped to give them a much better wedding and honeymoon.

Results

- The percentage who quit after brief advice may seem disappointingly low – often about 5%. But many succeed after repeated efforts.
- But if many doctors are doing it for all smokers the numbers of ex-smokers will be large.

■ The number of successes can be doubled or trebled with the use of nicotine substitutes, if available.

Nicotine replacement therapy (NRT)

Nicotine replacement therapy (NRT) has been shown to be more effective than other methods of doctor-assisted cessation. It is worth looking at this range of methods in more detail. (See also Raw et al., 1998; Simpson, 2000.)

The theory behind nicotine replacement is simple. The person trying to give up smoking gets nicotine temporarily (up to 8 weeks) in a pure, non-tobacco form, to relieve the craving that can accompany quitting. During this time they become gradually used to life as a non-smoker.

Types of NRT

There are five types of NRT: gum, patch, nasal spray, inhalator and sublingual tablets. Not all methods are licensed in all countries. The gum and patch have been available for longer and will probably be easier to get hold of.

■ The gum is available in 2 mg or 4 mg strengths. People can chew it when they feel they need it (e.g. whenever a cigarette would have been smoked), or at fixed times of the day. The gum tends to cause a medium blood-nicotine elevation compared with the high elevation of cigarette smoking.

■ The patch delivers nicotine to the bloodstream via the skin. It is usually worn on the upper arm, or the thigh or back. It gives a lower but relatively steady dose of nicotine all the time it is worn. It is either worn 24 hours a day or during waking hours only.

■ The gum and the patch may be used together. The patch sets up a relatively constant level of blood nicotine. The gum can be used to raise the level temporarily if the smoker gets a particular craving.

■ The nasal spray and the inhalator are used to respond to craving. They're more recent and have not yet been so carefully tested in practice.

■ The nicotine inhalator simulates smoking a cigarette. It consists of a plastic mouthpiece and a supply of nicotine cartridges that fit on the end. Despite its name, nicotine does not reach the lungs but is absorbed by the saliva in the mouth and throat, just like the gum (Raw et al., 1998).

■ Nicotine nasal spray consists of a small bottle of nicotine solution. The device is inserted into the nostril. A dose of nicotine is delivered when the top is pressed. This is the fastest way of absorbing nicotine, so it may help the more addicted smokers. However, the spray can irritate the nose and it can be difficult to get used to. Smokers who still experience severe craving in withdrawal with other products should try the spray (Raw et al., 1998).

- The sublingual tablets have the same mode of action as chewing gum but their use is less apparent and more aesthetic. They have not yet been fully tested in practice.

After reviewing available research, the UK's Cochrane Tobacco Addiction Group concluded:

- All these methods are effective in helping quitting.
- They increase success rates by two to three times in whatever setting they are used.
- They are best used in those who are motivated to quit and have a high nicotine addiction.
- There is little evidence about the value of NRT for people who smoke fewer than 10–15 cigarettes a day.
- Patches are easier to use in general practice when the doctor has only a short time with the patient. The doctor should use the other methods according to the patient's needs.
- Eight weeks of patch treatment is as effective as a longer course. Abrupt withdrawal of the patch is as effective as gradual withdrawal.
- Wearing a patch only during waking hours is as effective as wearing it for 24 hours a day
- Gum may be used either when the patient feels the need or on a fixed regular dose. Those who fail with 2-mg gum should be offered 4-mg gum.

When should NRT not be used?

Current opinion is that NRT is safer than smoking. Nevertheless many feel that it should not be used in pregnancy. In heart disease doctors should use their own judgement for each patient. Since quitting after a first heart attack makes a second one so much less likely, NRT may be justified, at least for certain patients.

What about the cost?

In countries where cigarettes are cheap, NRT may seem expensive. The doctor should emphasise that it is a temporary cost. In the long-term, patients who quit will save money. Even in low-income countries, there may be an influential minority, such as politicians, who can afford NRT.

In countries with high cigarette prices the cost of using NRT may be similar to the average cost of smoking over the same period. Doctors can use this to encourage patients to buy and use the treatment. Commercial competition may eventually reduce the costs of NRT.

How much support is needed with NRT?

The effectiveness of NRT does not seem to depend on the degree of additional support, but most trials have included at least some form of brief advice to the smoker (see page 61). Whether or not NRT needs a doctor's prescription varies from country to country. In some countries, e.g. UK, smokers can now buy most types of NRT direct from shops.

Other measures

- **Antidepressant drugs.** Buprion (also with commercial names Zyban, Amfebutamone or Wellbutrin in some countries) is sold in a slow-absorption form as an aid to quitting. Its use in quitting seems independent of its antidepressant effect. Results seem better if combined with NRT. But it can be used alone in patients who cannot tolerate NRT. It does require a doctor's prescription. It is best to give 150 mg each morning for 6 days before the patient starts to quit. A second dose of 150 mg, taken at least 8 hours after the first, is then added each day. Both should be taken for 7–9 weeks. Insomnia and dry mouth are common side-effects, especially when combined with NRT. A rare complication, convulsions, indicates that buprion should not be given to patients with epilepsy, alcoholism, brain disease, or those recently weaned from benzodiazepines or alcohol. Nortriptyline ('Nortrilen') seems also to increase the quit rate, but so far has not been well established.
- **Anxiolytics** (drugs to decrease anxiety). None has been shown to be effective.
- **Clonidine** (a drug to lower blood pressure). A few trials have shown that this drug helps but there are frequent side effects, including dry mouth and sleepiness. Not recommended.
- **Lobeline.** Long-term trials suggest it is not effective.
- **Acupuncture.** Only a placebo effect has been found.
- **Hypnosis.** No evidence of effectiveness found in controlled trials.

Physical measures

1. Expired (breathed out) carbon monoxide (CO) monitors show how much smoke the smoker has recently inhaled. Its use can encourage smokers to quit when they see how much CO is in their breath (and therefore their blood stream).
2. Saliva cotinine (a breakdown product of nicotine) can be measured accurately in a saliva specimen. This can be sent to the laboratory through the post. It is very useful for research purposes, or for verifying abstinence in 'Quit-and-Win' competitions (but obviously

no use in patients receiving NRT) – a smoker's claims to have stopped may not always be truthful.
3. Lung function machines can show smokers how much they have already damaged their lungs, and can encourage them to quit. Such devices are typically found in larger hospitals and chest clinics.

Special clinics

Special clinics can:

- give more intensive care to highly addicted smokers;
- train health professionals and others in how to help smokers quit;
- research ways, in each country and culture, to increase success in quitting.

Special clinics are expensive in professional time, but can be effective. Typically the smoker attends a weekly group session for several weeks – in general, the more weeks, the lower the relapse rate. Groups can motivate members and give mutual support. If available, NRT can double or treble the success rate. New anti-depressant drugs may be used.

The clinic need not be run by a doctor. A nurse or specially trained counsellor is cheaper and just as effective. Obviously enthusiasm and personality are important. A doctor's prescription may be necessary for antidepressants and some types of NRT.

Mrs Karlova had started smoking at the age of 12. At age 19, when she was smoking more than 20 cigarettes a day, she married a man who was also a heavy smoker. She had her first cigarette every day while still in bed in the morning. If she woke at night she had to have another one to get back to sleep. She smoked through her two pregnancies.

Then, aged 33, her husband developed a serious chronic illness. Mrs Karlova had to earn most of the family's money and felt she could not afford to smoke. Her mother and father gave her nicotine patches as a special present. Her doctor encouraged her and prescribed the patches. He saw her for several weeks to give her further support.

She developed acute bronchitis, but the doctor explained how this sometimes happens as a smoker's lungs start to clean themselves after years of heavy smoking. He prescribed an antibiotic and her cough soon disappeared. She felt much better and had more energy. She felt a great sense of achievement. Her husband managed to quit too. They are proud that there is now much less risk of the children becoming smokers.

Shortly after quitting, smokers with a cough sometimes find it more difficult to get up the phlegm. The irritation of cigarette smoke may previously have helped. They should be reassured that the cough will gradually improve as the constant irritation is withdrawn. Paradoxically, a few people with no previous cough while smoking, develop an acute cough when they stop. This is a good sign. The cilia – minute 'hairs' which normally help clear the bronchi (small tubes that carry air in the lungs) – have started working again.

In advising patients, it is worth mentioning that, on average, smoking each cigarette shortens a smoker's life by 11 minutes – a pack of 20 shortens it by 3 1/2 hours (i.e. a 20-a-day smoker loses about 3 1/2 hours every day, or one day of life every week).

Organising help in quitting

As a country's tobacco control programme builds, there should be a parallel increase in help for quitting (Slama, 1998).

At the initial stage, support services for cessation will be offered by individual doctors with a few special clinics run by enthusiasts.

Increasingly, training in counselling is becoming part of education for medical students. Counselling on smoking can be a very useful training exercise, and should form part of every medical student's education (Richmond, 1996).

Basic training should be extended to all health professionals. In due course every hospital should have a trained specialist or specialists to provide help to staff and patients. Cessation specialists need not be medically qualified. They should know about other facilities in their area to which they can refer hospital patients after discharge.

Advice on quitting should be available in all occupational health units. Employers and trade unions are increasingly aware of the need to encourage employees to quit. Motivation will build up as public education about tobacco increases, public places become routinely smoke free, and the media become supportive. Cessation support is especially important when workplaces are going smoke free.

Mr Ram Musa, a 40-year-old man, had been a farm worker. One year previously he had moved to the city in search of a better life. There he had worked in a factory. He was only paid a small wage that was not enough to give his family decent housing. He and his wife and three children lived in a hut he had built on waste ground.

For some years Mr Musa had had a smoker's cough that was worse in the morning. For the last 3 months his cough had grown more severe and he was more tired. His appetite became poorer. He thought he was getting thinner.

He first went to a local healer. The healer gave Mr Musa medicines and charged him a fee. But he got worse, not better. So Mr Musa went to a private doctor. The doctor gave him an antibiotic and charged him a fee. He went back to the doctor several times. Every time he returned, the doctor gave him other medicines and charged him more fees, but Mr Musa continued to get worse.

Finally, feeling very ill and having run out of money, he went to a government health centre where there was a well-trained Health Assistant (HA). In view of his symptoms the HA thought Mr Musa might have tuberculosis. He did the necessary investigations which confirmed tuberculosis. The HA then gave him the standard (free) treatment. When he returned for a check-up the HA explained that Mr Musa's smoking was bad for his health. If he stopped smoking it would help him to feel better quickly. It would give him more money to support his family. If he took his treatment regularly and stopped smoking he could continue to work. Otherwise the children would starve.

Mr Musa now had hope. He stopped smoking, took his treatment regularly, and soon lost his cough. He felt so much better that his work improved as well. He was given a better-paid job at the factory. He was also saving money by not smoking. Soon he was able to move his family into a better home.

So the Health Assistant had not only cured Mr Musa's tuberculosis. By persuading him to stop smoking, he speeded Mr Musa's recovery, saved him from other future diseases, and helped him out of poverty.

All schools, colleges and universities should offer cessation advice and support to staff and students, e.g. through school nurses, or, where available, health centres.

'Quit-lines' – telephone support services staffed by trained counsellors – are a vital part of provision in many countries. Some offer 24-hour help, others at particular times. In some countries, services are targeted at specific groups, e.g. pregnant women, or offered in minority languages. Internet or email-based advice is becoming increasingly common.

Cessation support can often be linked to particular dates, e.g. many people quit around New Year, or in relation to religious events such as Lent or Ramadan. Many countries have their own annual 'Quit Smoking Day', e.g. No Smoking Day (UK), Kick Butts Day and Great American Smoke Out (USA). The WHO's World No-Tobacco Day (May 31st every year) also gives an opportunity for large-scale publicity; therefore many countries adopt this day as their own special day for quitting.

A stepped approach to quitting services

Stepped approach to quitting services
Step 1. Health education and general information to increase motivation to quit.
Mass media.
Main effect on light smokers.

Step 2. Brief advice to quit from health professionals.
Main effect on light smokers.
Step 3. Advice, nicotine substitutes and follow-up appointment(s)
from health professionals.
Helps moderately motivated and addicted.
Step 4. Specialist clinics working with groups. Expensive.
Helps severely addicted.
Many smokers make repeated attempts and then relapse. They repeat
the cycles shown in Figure. 7.2.

Figure 7.2 The process of stopping smoking.

As the knowledge and climate of opinion about smoking build up in a country, the demand for help in quitting will grow. The levels of help should be the most appropriate and cost-effective.

Step 1 depends on the gradual build-up of public opinion. Where there has been no public concern, it will at first be the lone voices of pioneers that are heard. Later it will be public action by voluntary or government associations, and then (one hopes) by the government using legislation.

Step 2 can start early among pioneer doctors. It can then gradually spread to all doctors and health professionals. There will be many failures, but if many professionals act, even with a small percentage success rate, the number of ex-smokers in the country will grow.

Step 3 depends on whether nicotine replacement therapies (NRT) are available and can be afforded.

Mr Inez was a wealthy politician aged 43. He had been a heavy smoker for many years. His wife did not smoke. One winter his wife developed a very bad cold. She worsened and developed a high fever. Mr Inez called in their doctor. The doctor diagnosed pneumonia and put her on an antibiotic. He came back to see her every few days as she gradually improved.

The doctor was one of the small group in that country who had realised the increasing threat of tobacco. The habit was spreading rapidly because of major advertising by international tobacco companies. He had noted when visiting Mrs Inez that Mr Inez also had a cough. He asked him about this and about his smoking. Mr Inez said it was 'just a smoker's cough'. The doctor said he would give him a check-up. He found he had early signs of bronchitis. He explained the dangers to Mr Inez and warned him that he might get increasingly breathless if he continued smoking. His cough would get worse, he risked developing pneumonia, and he might go on to get lung cancer. The doctor added that Mrs Inez might have got her pneumonia because she was exposed to so much smoke in the home, and that their children might also be affected.

With all these warnings, for the sake of his wife and children's health as well as his own, Mr Inez decided he would make the attempt.

The doctor heard that Mr Inez smoked 25 cigarettes a day, the first as soon as he woke in the morning. He was obviously severely addicted. Nicotine substitutes (NRT) had just become available in the country. Mr Inez could well afford the cost. As he was an influential politician if he could be cured of his smoking he would probably influence others and might save many lives.

So the doctor prescribed NRT. He saw and encouraged Mr Inez regularly. Mrs Inez gave her husband great support. Mr Inez, a strong character, managed to come off cigarettes. It was tough but the NRT certainly helped.

Mr Inez was so delighted with his success that he agreed to become a member of the group pushing for government and public action on smoking. He proved a splendid ally.

At first, activists might concentrate on motivated opinion-formers, such as politicians, who can afford nicotine substitutes. Where cigarettes are expensive, the cost of the substitutes may be less forbidding. However, there has been a great increase in competition between pharmaceutical companies to sell nicotine substitutes. In due course, prices may fall.

Step 4. Specialist clinics are expensive in time and manpower. Pioneer clinics may serve a limited number of the severely addicted. But they can also be training centres to teach others, and settings for research.

In industrialised countries it has been suggested that about 20% of all smokers might be treated with nicotine substitutes at Step 3 and 5% at Step 4 (Foulds, 1996).

Conclusions

Physical addiction and social/psychological habituation means quitting is difficult for many smokers. Yet over the years millions of people, who formerly smoked heavily, have succeeded in quitting. As public opinion in a country gradually recognises the dangers, more and more people will want to stop.

Most quitters have been light or moderate smokers. Nicotine substitutes are a major advance for the more-addicted smoker. Pharmaceutical firms now realise the enormous potential, so competition is increasing variety and availability of products, and also lowering prices. In their own interest, manufacturers will be increasingly effective in promoting quitting. They should also prove useful allies in funding, for example, meetings and anti-smoking campaigns. As always, there must be caution to ensure that drug company support is used strictly ethically and not primarily for immediate commercial gain.

Antidepressant drugs may work well to help the more severely addicted to quit. These drugs should only be used in addition to nicotine substitutes, and must only be prescribed under medical control.

With such enormous potential demand there is much current research to find new quitting aids. There may be further important advances in the next few years.

Appendix 7.1: The Fagerstrom Index for Nicotine Dependence

This is a more elaborate test, mainly used in special cessation clinics and research projects. The test gives a score for the degree of addiction: the higher the score, the greater the addiction. The maximum score is 10. A score of more than 7 means that the person is very addicted and will find it difficult to give up smoking. (Scores are given in brackets after each answer.)

1. How soon after waking do you smoke your first cigarette?
   Within 5 minutes (3)
   6–30 minutes (2)
   31–60 minutes (1)
   60+ minutes (0)
2. Do you find it difficult not smoking in places where it is forbidden e.g. church, library, cinema etc?
   Yes (1)
   No (0)
3. Which cigarette would you find it most difficult to give up?
   The first one in the morning (1) All others (0)

4. How many cigarettes do you smoke a day?
> 10 or fewer (0)
> 11–20 (1)
> 21–30 (2)
> 31+ (3)

5. Do you smoke more frequently during the first hour after waking than in the rest of the day?
> Yes (1)
> No (0)

6. Do you smoke when so ill that you are in bed most of the day?
> Yes (1)
> No (0)

Interpretation

0–2	not dependant
3–4	mildly dependant
5–6	moderately dependant
7–8	strongly dependant
9–10	very strongly dependant

General references

Fiore MC, Bailey WC, Cohen SJ et al. 1996. Smoking cessation. Clinical Practice Guideline No.18. Rockville: Agency for Health Care Policy and Research, US Department of Health and Human Services, Publication No. 96-0692.
Primarily addressed to an American audience but much of it applicable elsewhere.

Foulds J. 1996. Strategies for smoking cessation. Br Med Bull 52(1): 157–173.
A useful review of work up to that time, mainly based on research in industrialised countries.

Raw M, McNeill A, West R. 1998. Smoking cessation guidelines for health professionals. Thorax 53 (Suppl 5, Part 1): S1–S17.
Primarily addressed to the National Health Service in UK but a very useful guide for others.

Richmond R (ed.). 1994. Interventions for smokers. An international perspective. Baltimore: Williams and Wilkins. ISBN 0-683-07272-2.
A comprehensive review of practice, largely based on work in Europe, North America and Australia.

Richmond R (ed.). 1996. Educating medical students about tobacco: planning and implementation. Paris: International Union against Tuberculosis and Lung Disease. ISBN 0-646-314971.

Covers how and what medical students should be taught about tobacco. Also how to introduce and organise this teaching in a medical school. Examples from China, India, Turkey, South Africa, Japan and Egypt.

Simpson D. 2000. Doctors and tobacco. A guide for European medical associations. London: Tobacco Control Resources Centre at British Medical Association. ISBN 0-7279-1491-X

Slama K. 1998. Tobacco control and prevention. A guide for low-income countries. Paris: International Union against Tuberculosis and Lung Disease.

Includes useful model forms and questionnaires on quitting.

8 | Action by Doctors and Other Health Professionals

In this chapter we concentrate on the specific opportunities and responsibilities of doctors and other health professionals regarding tobacco. These aspects of tobacco control are summarised in the box below.

> **Why doctors should get involved in tobacco control**
> - In many countries much of a doctor's time is spent with patients suffering from tobacco-related diseases.
> - Getting involved with tobacco control, either as an individual or through groups, societies etc. gives an opportunity to do something about *the* biggest preventable cause of suffering and death.
> - Most people regard doctors as the most reliable source of knowledge and advice on matters of health.
> - The doctor's example has an important influence on the rest of the community. Doctors should not smoke themselves.

Doctors can help to protect their patients, and patients' families, by timely warning of tobacco's dangers. They can help patients to stop smoking – especially those patients who have tobacco-related illnesses. They can use their immense influence in their local and national communities to encourage tobacco control measures. Doctors' organisations should seek to work with a wide range of other relevant bodies (p 120). Such joint action has proved very effective.

Personal example

It has been said that a smoking doctor is worth US$100,000 to the tobacco companies, because the bad example set by doctors who smoke may make some smokers think that smoking cannot be as dangerous as they have been told. In many countries only low numbers of doctors now smoke. It is important to publicise this: surveys have often shown that children and many adults in the community imagine that more

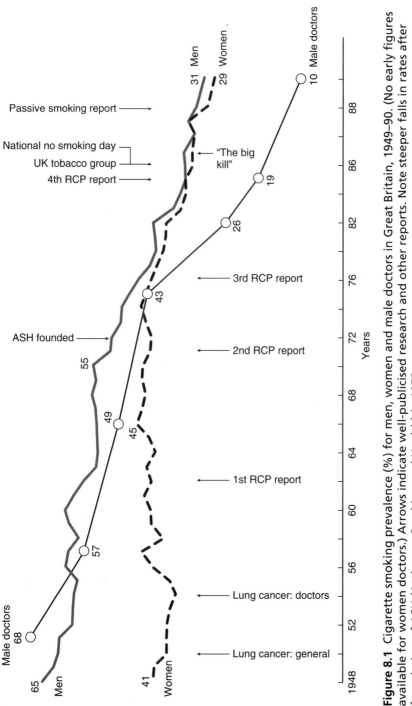

Figure 8.1 Cigarette smoking prevalence (%) for men, women and male doctors in Great Britain, 1949–90. (No early figures available for women doctors.) Arrows indicate well-publicised research and other reports. Note steeper falls in rates after foundation of ASH (Action on Smoking and Health) in 1972.

doctors smoke than is actually the case. Figure 8.1 shows the cigarette smoking trends in male doctors in Great Britain from 1948 to 1990, compared with the national trends in men and women. If you can find similar differences between doctors and the general population in your country, give them wide publicity.

Responsibilities to patients

- As a routine all patients, whatever their health problem, should be asked whether they smoke. The details should be recorded in the notes. Smoking may well be related to the medical problem or to treating it, e.g. post-operative complications are more common in smokers.
- If the medical problem may be related to smoking, the doctor should raise the problem of stopping. For details of the best approaches to this see Chapter 7.
- Even if the medical problem is not related to smoking, the doctor should raise the question of stopping. Patients' replies will indicate how willing they are to consider this. Again, for details see Chapter 7.
- When parents bring their children to the doctor, the doctor should raise the question of the parents' smoking and its possible effect on their children (see Chapter 6 and the box below). For appropriate age groups, the doctor should also approach the child.

A 'contract' or agreement to stay tobacco-free

The parents offer the pre-teenage child a reward (appearing substantial to the child) for not smoking until a certain age, e.g. 18 or 21 years. There should be careful discussion why the parents are keen to save the child from smoking. There should be arrangements for discussing any temporary lapse.

A contract like this can have an effect on the child's peers. The child can be envied for having this reward to look forward to, so other children may be less likely to press him or her to smoke.

- Always discuss smoking in antenatal interviews. See Chapter 5.
- Many children start smoking in their teens. The doctor should raise the problem with every teenage patient and give appropriate advice – to consider stopping or, if a non-smoker, not to start. In some general practices in western countries the doctor tries to see most teenagers to advise them about health matters as they grow up. This would include discussion of lifestyle issues, e.g. smoking, alcohol, sex, drugs etc.

Figure 8.2 (Reproduced with kind permission of Ms Calman)

The medical environment

The aim should be to make all medical environments smoke free. The speed with which this is done will depend on the local climate of opinion about smoking. It is useful to do an initial survey of staff. Ask both about their smoking habits and their attitude towards having smoke-free premises. Opinion in favour of smoke-free premises is often more widespread than expected. This would encourage managers to bring in a smoke-free policy. In the early stage it is worth providing a room where smokers can go to smoke. It is also important to provide help for staff members who wish to stop.

Figure 8.3

In hospitals it is worth discussing with staff members whether there should be a room where patients' visitors (especially worried visitors to very ill or dying patients) can smoke. Also whether there should be initial provision of a smoking room for patients. This is perhaps particularly important in psychiatric hospitals where smoking is often widespread among patients.

As local and community opinion becomes increasingly convinced of the value of a smoke-free atmosphere, it may be possible to withdraw these special provisions for smokers.

Education and training

Medical students

For details see Richmond (1996), which also includes a brief checklist of action – this is summarised below. This need not be an additional burden on the curriculum, but will help to ensure that relevant tobacco aspects are covered by the many specialties concerned.

All students should have training in counselling. Counselling patients on tobacco can provide a convenient introduction to counselling methods.

Suggested action within the medical school

- Appoint a coordinator of tobacco education.
- Consider an initial survey of:
- medical students' habits, knowledge and attitudes: suitable questionnaires can be obtained from the World Health Organization or the International Union against Tuberculosis and Lung Disease (see Appendix B);
- staff attitudes – design a questionnaire locally.
- The coordinator should produce a written policy in consultation with relevant colleagues covering:
- smoke-free medical school premises and hospitality areas;
- teaching in relevant departments: checklist for each department (see Richmond, 1996);
- examinations: ensure tobacco problems are covered in theoretical and clinical examinations (particularly ensure that the student has always taken a smoking history);
- methods proposed for monitoring students' progress;
- the value of giving a brief talk to new medical students on their first day in the faculty. Explain the importance of smoking as a major preventable cause of disease and the importance of their personal example as doctors and non-smokers.
- Carry out a formal review to assess progress one to two years after the start of the programme.

Continuing medical education

Tobacco should be a component in all relevant postgraduate education. There should be sessions at meetings of all relevant specialist societies, e.g. national medical associations (Simpson, 2000), oncology, cardiology, respiratory medicine, obstetrics, paediatrics, public health, occupational health. Similar policies should apply to dentists and dental students. All scientific meetings should be smoke free. There should be regular reviews of national statistics, policy and progress on tobacco and tobacco-related illnesses in relevant medical journals.

Figure 8.4 (Reproduced with kind permission of the Turkish Medical Association)

The local community

With their high prestige in health matters, doctors can give valuable support to action in local communities such as:

- campaigns for smoke-free clinics, hospitals, schools, restaurants, offices, public transport, leisure areas and workplaces;
- a special day to encourage and help people to stop smoking, often part of a national campaign;
- a campaign to persuade local (region, county, town or village) authorities to ban advertising on their property;
- campaigns to prevent sales of cigarettes to children;
- campaigns against local tobacco-sponsored events, e.g. sports, fashion shows, discos etc.

Doctors' comments in local press or broadcast media can be particularly helpful. Doctors should emphasise that their only vested interest is in people's health – in contrast to tobacco companies!

Figure 8.5 (Reproduced with kind permission of the Turkish Medical Association)

Personalising: The doctor's personal, recent experience impresses, for example:

- *'Only this morning I saw a patient who ...'*
- *'In every clinic I see patients needlessly suffering ...'*
- *'I keep on having to admit patients to scarce hospital beds because of entirely preventable conditions ...'*

This sort of approach helps people to understand the problem.

Politicians

Meeting politicians

It is always most effective to meet a politician personally. Most politicians will accept an invitation to a clinic or hospital. This can be particularly valuable when a campaign is starting. Introduce the politician to relevant specialists. Arrange to have a photograph taken and invite the media: the publicity is good for the politician and good for the campaign (and good for shaming the politician later if he or she supports tobacco!).

'The full force of medical opinion'
How a politician may perceive letters from doctors:
- *One letter:* ' A letter from a doctor'.
- *Two doctors' letters on the same topic:* 'There seems to be increasing concern among doctors'
- *Three doctors' letters:* 'This is obviously what the medical profession thinks about this issue.'

Doctors as professional advisors

Public health

Preventing the most preventable cause of premature death must have high priority for all public health doctors. All sections of this book are relevant to their activities.

Occupational health

Persuade management that the health and efficiency of their employees will greatly benefit from:
- helping smokers to quit (less illness, less time off work)
- developing smoke-free work areas.

This may have to be a gradual process: see notes on smoke-free hospitals p 105.

National action by doctors

Doctors and their National Medical Associations will have a major part to play in national campaigning (Chapter 12) to establish a national tobacco control programme and appropriate legislation (Chapter 10). For more detailed guidance, addressed to national medical associations see Simpson (2000). Although this was written primarily for European national medical associations, many of its recommendations are widely applicable.

Nurses and other health workers

Why nurses and other health workers?

- They are greatly respected by the general public. Of course all health professionals should set a good example by not smoking themselves.

Figure 8.6 Doctors played an important role in influencing public opinion before Sweden's Tobacco Act was adopted in 1993.

- They often spend more time with patients than doctors, giving opportunity for informal advice.
- Patients often find it easier to ask questions and discuss their problems with nurses and other health workers.
- Community nurses and other community health workers often visit families at home. They can influence and advise parents and children.

The training of nurses and other health workers should cover tobacco problems. As with medical students, advising patients on smoking can be a training exercise when teaching students how to counsel patients. In some countries there is concern about the number of nurses who smoke. There is evidence that this is lower when nursing students have had education about tobacco.

Dentists

Both tobacco smoking and oral tobacco cause damage to mouth and teeth. Dentists are therefore in a strong position to advise against smoking and to encourage smokers to stop. They can have a particular influence on parents and children.

Professions allied to medicine

Physiotherapists, occupational therapists, radiographers and other health professionals all have opportunities to influence patients. They should have basic training on tobacco problems and should be encouraged to use that knowledge in advising patients.

Non-professional hospital and clinic staff

Many of these people have opportunities to chat with patients informally while making beds, wheeling patients on trolleys etc. They can be useful allies in creating a climate of opinion against smoking. We believe that much can be gained by encouraging this sort of activity. It can be rewarding for the staff if they feel they are helping patients and contributing to an important health campaign.

General references

Glynn TJ, Manley MW, Mecklenburg R. 1994. Involvement of physicians and dentists in smoking cessation: a public health perspective. In Richmond R (ed.). Interventions for smokers. An international perspective. London: Williams and Wilkins. ISBN 0-683-07272-2.
A comprehensive review of practice, largely based on work in Europe, Australia and USA.

Richmond R (ed.). 1996. Educating medical students about tobacco: planning and implementation. Paris: International Union against Tuberculosis and Lung Disease. ISBN 0-646-314971.
Covers what medical students should be taught about tobacco. Also how to introduce and organise teaching in a medical school.
Examples from China, India, Turkey, South Africa, Japan and Egypt.

Simpson D. 2000. Doctors and tobacco. Medicine's Big Challenge. London: Tobacco Control Resource Centre at British Medical Association. ISBN 0-7279-1491-X.
Written for Europe but most of it applicable for many countries.

9 | Tobacco Industry

The tobacco industry is a collection of companies of very different size and significance. Some are local or national, some state-owned, but the biggest and most powerful are a few huge multinationals that work on a global scale. Like any corporation, they strive to increase market share and profitability on behalf of their shareholders. Not surprisingly, the industry strongly resists any measures designed to reduce consumption of tobacco. Their resistance may be open and public. Even more dangerously it is often secret and indirect.

In this chapter we give a brief account of the tobacco industry, especially the multinationals. Methods used by the industry to increase its already enormous sales and profits have been mentioned throughout this book. For convenience we summarise them here. We outline the claims made by the industry of its financial value to governments, and the World Bank's criticism of these claims. Finally, we review the economic cost of the tobacco habit to governments and the World Bank's assessment of the cost-effectiveness of tobacco control.

National health/National wealth

The tobacco industry has a profoundly destructive effect on a nation's wealth as well as its health.

- Tobacco-related diseases are an immense cost to a country. A high proportion of people who die from these diseases are of working age. Patients, bereaved partners, and orphans have to be cared for, either by their families or by the state.
- Imported cigarettes, whether legal or smuggled, are a major drain on a country's foreign exchange reserves.
- In many countries a high proportion of fires in homes, public buildings and transport are caused by smoking. Cigarettes are a notorious cause of forest fires.
- Cleaning costs are much higher in buildings and public transport where smoking is permitted. Cigarette packets and butts form a

major part of the rubbish dropped on streets and other public places.

- Tobacco crops may occupy land that would be better used for growing food. In countries where wood is used for 'curing' tobacco, trees may be cut down and not replaced, or land may be restocked inappropriately. Deforestation may reduce rainfall and spread deserts, and add to the burdens of poor people.
- The World Bank's 1993 World Development Report 'Investing in Health' concludes that tobacco control policies are cost-effective and should be included in any health care programme.
- Raising prices by increasing tax on tobacco is by far the most cost-effective measure of improving a nation's health, and even earns money for the government. In terms of years of life saved it is more effective than many other health interventions (even child immunisation).
- Workers who smoke can be expensive. A recent study estimated that British businesses lost £100 million a week in lost minutes for breaks, absences from work due to smoking-related illness, and fire damage caused by carelessly discarded cigarettes. A number of firms now only hire non-smokers, and in some cases pay non-smokers more than smokers.

Big tobacco

Apart from China (see below), the world's tobacco trade is dominated by a small number of multinational tobacco companies, including Philip Morris, British American Tobacco (BAT), and Japan Tobacco (Table 9.1).

The largest member of Big Tobacco is Philip Morris, ranked 70th among the world's wealthiest corporations in 1998. Its key brand is Marlboro, the world's biggest-selling brand and the one most aggressively promoted. In 1998, Philip Morris had an annual revenue of US$74 billion –US$49 billion from tobacco (other parts of its empire include Kraft Foods, the Miller brewery, and – since late 2000 – Nabisco). This is larger than the total economic activity of many developing countries.

BAT is now much the same size as Philip Morris, having taken over Rothmans in 1999. The combined BAT has 97 factories operating in 66 countries and produces over 800 billion cigarettes per year. Having been strong for many years in Asia, South America and Africa, BAT is now expanding into eastern Europe and ex-USSR. BAT prides itself on its diversity of brands targeted at different groups. There are numerous local brands, currently accounting for three-quarters of its global sales, but its key international brands are growing fast. These include Dunhill,

Table 9.1 Top 21 Tobacco companies 1999

		HQ	Billion cigarettes
1	China National Tobacco Corporation	China	>1600
2	Philip Morris	US	>800
3	British American Tobacco (BAT)	UK	>800
4	Japan Tobacco	Japan	>400
5	Tabakprom	Russia	<100
6	Altadis	France/Spain	<100
7	RJ Reynolds	US	<100
8	KT&G	S Korea	<100
9	Tekel	Turkey	<100
10	Reemtsma	Germany	<100
11	Gudang Garam	Indonesia	<100
12	ITC	India	<100
13	AAMS	Italy	<100
14	Imperial Tobacco	UK	<100
15	Lorillard	US	<100
16	TTM	Thailand	<100
17	Gallaher	UK	<100
18	Fortune Tobacco	Philippines	<100
19	HMS	Indonesia	<100
20	Austria Tobacco	Austria	<100
21	Taiwan Monopoly	Taiwan	<100

Source: Goldman Sachs Global Equity Research

Lucky Strike, Kent, State Express 555, Rothmans, Peter Stuyvesant, Benson & Hedges, Kool, Pall Mall, Viceroy, Winfield and John Player Gold Leaf.

Japan Tobacco Inc. (JTI) is a former national monopoly. It was privatised some years ago, but the Japanese government continues to hold the majority of its shares. It has recently taken over the overseas interests of the major US-based company, RJ Reynolds, and is set to play an increasing part in world markets.

We should add that the Chinese national tobacco monopoly (which has been forging links with US and British companies) is now also a major exporter to Asian countries. In the same way, India's ITC, part owned by BAT, is itself moving into foreign markets.

Other large companies that operate internationally are Reemtsma (Germany) and Altadis – formed after a merger between Seita (France) and Tabacalera (Spain).

The world strategy of the multinationals

- In the last 50 years, the efforts of anti-tobacco campaigners have resulted in declining tobacco markets in North America, Europe (especially Northern Europe) and Australasia.
- Consequently, the multinationals have switched to building markets in developing countries and in the newly opened markets of Central and Eastern Europe and the former USSR. The expanding economies of some Asian countries have been particularly attractive.
- The low rate of smoking among women in many developing countries is seen as a great opportunity to expand in those markets, using advertising and other promotional tactics. For more details see Chapter 5.

Major threats to the tobacco companies

The multinationals are not having it all their own way. They face various obstacles to expansion into new markets. These include restraints on trade and advertising, and a growing understanding among the world's peoples of what the tobacco companies are up to.

- The tobacco industry is particularly concerned about the scientific evidence of the dangers of environmental tobacco smoke (ETS) (see Chapter 3). In many countries this is having a major effect on public opinion, increasing restrictions on public smoking, which reduce sales and erode the social acceptability of smoking.
- The publicity given to previously secret company documents, which reveal massive misconduct by the companies (see Chapter 11). The public is becoming increasingly aware of the companies' ruthless methods.
- Publicity on the high priority now given to countering tobacco by the World Health Organization, with the Framework Convention on Tobacco Control, unanimously passed by the World Health Assembly in May 2003.

Although these factors are now dominating much public opinion in Western countries, the tobacco industry is doing its best to confuse and obscure them in their developing markets elsewhere.

Figure 9.1

Figure 9.2 (Reproduced with kind permission of Tribune Media Services, Chicago)

How multinationals displace national tobacco monopolies

A number of countries operate national tobacco monopolies. 'Western' cigarettes tend to have high prestige in such countries, but are often very expensive and in short supply. In some cases they are excluded altogether. Multinationals are keen to overwhelm national monopolies and shoulder their way into local markets.

Multinationals have used international treaties promoting free trade (mostly sponsored by the World Trade Organization and its predecessor) and powerful political pressure (in the past, from the US government and individual senators) to ensure that they can market their brands universally, and that the taxes levied are no higher than on domestic brands.

The next stage is often to make 'joint venture' agreements with the national tobacco company to give technical assistance in manufacture in return for the right to produce their own 'Western' brands locally. Later, the foreign company can use its position to press for more freedom to operate entirely independently. This is one way of getting into a country 'by the back door'.

Multinationals then plead that only full access to the market will reduce smuggling, and make it possible for governments to collect all taxes (see Box below for comments).

This argument is complete hypocrisy, of course. Smuggling is one of the main ways multinationals penetrate national markets. Since they pay no duties or sales taxes on smuggled cigarettes, the price of their brands is kept artificially low. Smuggling on the present massive scale can only take place with the active assistance of the multinationals. As we write, this is the subject of several court cases and government investigations.

How the multinationals use smuggling to penetrate closed markets

According to Professor Elif Dagli, head of a department of paediatric chest disease in Istanbul, Turkey, the multinationals have a clear strategy:

1. They install a factory in a neighbouring country to promote smuggling (in Turkey's case the factory was in Bulgaria).
2. Once they have significantly promoted smuggling, they lobby to obtain the right to legally export cigarettes (that would take care of the smuggling problem!).
3. They lobby to abolish any existing tobacco control law, especially concerning advertising and promotion.
4. They increase consumption by targeting youth and women with heavy advertising and promotion.

5. They push for the privatisation of the former monopoly.
6. They buy out the former monopoly. Turkey is now in phase 4.

> Source: Professor Elif Dagli was speaking at the 11th World Conference on Tobacco or Health in Chicago in August 2000.

How the multinationals oppose tobacco control measures

Denial of health effects

The tobacco industry habitually denies or tries to cast doubt on the evidence for health damage by smoking. For many years the industry argued that damage by active smoking had not been proved, claiming that 'more research is necessary'. Recently the companies seem to be admitting some of the dangers of active smoking, though such admissions tend to be on their Internet websites, to which most people in developing countries do not have access. Furthermore, the admissions are carefully worded, using evasive phrases such as 'medical authorities say smoking may cause serious disease', rather than fully endorsing this themselves.

But the companies have dug in their heels over environmental tobacco smoke (ETS). The industry clearly sees evidence that ETS harms non-smokers as a major threat to its existence. Every restriction on the right to smoke in public places cuts consumption, lowers public acceptance of smoking, and increases the likelihood that smokers will quit for good.

Hence companies have employed tame scientists and statisticians to deny or deliberately underestimate risk; and promoted their views through specially staged symposia on 'indoor air pollution' or 'sick building syndrome'. Since the illusion of objectivity counts for so much, the companies typically take great pains to conceal that they have sponsored and organised these events and packed them with their own spokesmen.

Sometimes such a symposium even attracts reputable scientists who use them to voice dissenting views. But in practice the published report of the proceedings will typically play down their contributions. Much greater publicity is given to the industry-sponsored scientists who focus on non-tobacco sources of pollution, and who neglect or attack evidence for the ill effects of ETS.

The tobacco industry promotes 'Smokers' Rights' organisations

These often claim to be independent but are in fact funded by the industry. They attack tobacco control measures as the work of 'health fascists' and the 'nanny state'. Anti-smoking activists or organisations may be threatened with libel actions (see p 112).

Advertising
Tobacco companies claim that advertising does not increase consumption, but merely encourages smokers to 'switch brands'. This is simply not plausible, since advertising budgets are immense and few smokers switch brands. The industry fights against advertising restrictions more fiercely than against perhaps any other measure.

In countries with restrictions on advertising, companies have a range of other marketing tricks up their sleeves, including 'brand stretching' (promoting other non-tobacco goods and services with the same name and brand image as their cigarette brands). They also sponsor a wide range of activities, including sports, arts, science and scientists, academics, and even charities.

Children
Companies say they are against smoking by children. They claim their advertising is not directed at children and that it has no effect on them. They even fund educational programmes, allegedly to persuade children not to smoke until they are adult. In fact, they are worthless programmes whose aim is to prevent other measures being taken which might be more effective. The industry youth programmes may even encourage smoking by promoting the notion that smoking is 'adult' – a sure attraction to rebellious young people.

Journalists
The industry seeks to influence journalists to produce favourable 'independent' articles, notably on environmental tobacco smoke. For example, BAT organises briefings for selected journalists in developing countries, using 'experts' from the West, to try to 'balance' the 'debate' about smoking. Their views are, of course, consistent with tobacco industry propaganda.

Politicians
Tobacco companies routinely fund political parties and politicians. They often back all the leading parties, to maintain their position whichever party wins the election.

Governments
Powerful international pressure is put on governments if they do not allow imports of foreign cigarettes or tax them highly. Examples include Japan, Taiwan, Thailand and South Korea.

For examples of the tobacco industry's efforts to prevent legislation, mainly in the USA, see Sweda and Daynard (1996).

The tobacco industry opposes tobacco control as a 'threat to a nation's economy'

As we indicate in the box on page 85, the tobacco industry is immensely damaging to a nation's economy. Yet the industry often claims that it is tobacco *control*, particularly taxes, that is the more serious risk. They allege a range of dire consequences, among them that:

1. 'Unemployment will grow.' It almost certainly will not. The industry commonly exaggerates the numbers they employ, so fewer workers are in fact at risk.

   Already, tobacco manufacture is highly mechanised and needs little manpower – the industry itself made most tobacco workers redundant years ago. In most countries it accounts for less than 1% of manufacturing jobs (the figures are a little higher in Turkey, Bangladesh, Egypt, Philippines, and Thailand).

   In some countries, tobacco farming does indeed employ substantial numbers (though industry propaganda often inflates the figures by counting all members of a farmer's family as employed). But many farmers also grow other crops anyway, or could switch production to another cash crop.

   In practice, tobacco farming is unlikely to drop significantly until there is substantial world decrease in tobacco consumption (see discussion on p109).

   Indeed, tobacco control should actually *increase* employment. The World Bank points out that when tobacco consumption decreases, people spend their money on other goods that need more labour to produce so employment grows in those sectors. Research in the USA and UK confirms this. A World Bank study concluded that in Bangladesh numbers of jobs would increase by 18% if smokers spent their money on other goods and services.

2. 'Higher tax will reduce government revenues.' Yes – when smoking disappears. But in the short and medium term, revenues will rise. Fewer cigarettes may be smoked, but the tax yield will be higher. The World Bank (World Bank, 1999) calculates that, worldwide, a 10% increase in tobacco tax would result in a 5% cut in cigarette consumption but a 7% increase in the tax revenue to governments (see Figure 10.1, p 101).

3. 'Higher taxes will cause a massive increase in smuggling.' In fact, the level of taxation alone cannot explain smuggling, and reducing taxes certainly will not reduce smuggling. Many high-tax countries have very low smuggling rates, and vice versa. The serious problem is not bootlegging – legally buying tobacco in a low-tax country and illegally reselling it in a high-tax country – but large-scale organised smuggling on which no taxes are paid. This sort of smuggling is impossible without the collusion of the tobacco companies who

supply the cigarettes. If governments ensure the companies are fully accountable for taxes, contraband sales will plummet.

In any case, an increase in the smuggling of cheap cigarettes is unlikely to increase total consumption or reduce tax revenue. The World Bank concludes from studies in many high-income countries that consumption will still fall and governments will still gain more in tax income. Some of the increased income can be used to control smuggling (see also Chapter 10).

Table 9.2 Top 20 Tobacco growers 2000

	Production of tobacco leaves (metric tonnes)	Country
	6,963,716	World
1	2,509,972	China
2	701,700	India
3	594,322	Brazil
4	498,900	United States of America
5	261,890	Turkey
6	227,726	Zimbabwe
7	137,564	Indonesia
8	132,200	Italy
9	129,900	Greece
10	120,000	Malawi
11	113,400	Argentina
12	108,800	Pakistan
13	74,200	Thailand
14	72,000	Canada
15	71,090	Philippines
16	65,443	Korea. Republic of
17	64,000	Japan
18	62,000	Korea. Dem People's Rep
19	46,260	Myanmar
20	46,000	Laos

Source: FAO. (www.FAO.org)

4. 'Increased taxes make poor consumers poorer.' This would be true if people continued to smoke as much as they did before. But they don't. Evidence shows that a rise in tax results in a bigger decrease in consumption among poor consumers than richer ones. Governments should use some of the increased revenue from tobacco to help smokers to quit. (See Chapter 7.)

Conclusions

■ The multinational tobacco companies, with their vast resources of finance and marketing skills, are a major threat to world health.
■ In addition to ill-health, the tobacco habit poses a great social and financial burden on individuals, societies and governments.
■ The World Bank has concluded that tobacco control benefits a nation's wealth as well as its health. Governments can be reassured of its cost-effectiveness.

References

Mackay J, Crofton J. 1996. Tobacco and the developing world. Br Med Bull 52(1): 206–221.
Includes a brief history of the tobacco industry's activities, especially related to Asia.
Pollock D. 1996. Forty years on: a war to recognise and win. How the tobacco industry has survived the revelations on tobacco and health. Br Med Bull 52(1): 174–182.
Mainly an account of how a major multinational company has successfully avoided tobacco control for such a long time.
Simpson D. 2000. Doctors and tobacco. London: Tobacco Control Resource Centre at British Medical Association. ISBN 0-7279-1491-X.
Sweda EL Jr, Daynard RA. 1996. Tobacco industry tactics. Br Med Bull 52(1): 183-192.
Mainly recounts tobacco industry tactics in the USA.
World Bank. 1999. Curbing the epidemic. Governments and the economics of tobacco control. Washington DC: World Bank. ISBN 0-8213-4519-2.
An excellent and readable report. Very useful to quote.

10 National Tobacco Control Programmes

In this chapter we shall examine in some detail the main elements of any national tobacco control programme. We shall say something about problems and difficulties in developing and implementing such a programme, and suggest how they may be overcome. The main strategies for building favourable public opinion will be discussed in Chapter 12 Campaigning.

As we write, the World Health Organization is consulting widely with the aim of developing a formal international agreement on the essential elements of any national tobacco control programme. Findings will be incorporated in a Framework Convention on Tobacco Control (FCTC). After recommendation by the World Health Assembly, countries will be invited to sign the Convention committing them to implement the Convention in their national law. (This is much the same process as led to the United Nations Framework Convention on Climate Change by which countries agreed to reduce their carbon dioxide outputs to reduce 'global warming'.)

A strong Framework Convention is highly desirable, but may take some years to achieve (though it is intended to be ready for signing by the year 2003). Meanwhile the publicity and international discussions are likely to influence public opinion in many countries. This will make it easier for health advocates to persuade their governments to take action, even before the government signs up to the Convention.

National tobacco control policy
Most experts now agree that the outlines of any national tobacco control policy should cover all of the following areas, and must be backed by close monitoring and tough, strictly enforced legislation:
- a ban on all tobacco promotion (advertising, sponsorship etc.);
- increasing prices through taxation;
- public education and information programmes;
- strong, prominent health warnings;
- smoke-free public places;
- reduced toxicity of tobacco smoke;

- support for smoking cessation (quitting);
- a ban on tobacco sales to children;
- phasing out of tobacco-growing;
- using criminal and civil law against tobacco companies;
- regular monitoring and evaluation of progress.

Legislation or voluntary agreement?

Since a successful tobacco control policy means a fall in sales and profits for tobacco companies, they use more or less any means to obstruct progress. They always oppose legislation and suggest instead 'self-regulation' as a 'fairer' or 'easier' alternative, or sometimes they suggest legislation that they know will not work.

How 'voluntary agreement' and 'self-regulation' are supposed to work

The government and the tobacco companies together shape and agree a set of regulations. These usually cover ways in which cigarettes may be advertised and what health warnings they should carry. The companies say they will operate within these regulations; in return, the government agrees not to introduce stronger controls or legislation.

Wherever this has been tried, 'self-regulation' has never worked effectively. The companies always find ways of getting round any agreements.

- It takes many meetings to negotiate the formal agreements. This gives the companies plenty of time to plan how to get round them.
- Agreements are never comprehensive. All sorts of methods of promotion, including some not yet used, may be overlooked in the agreement.
- Several different departments of government are usually involved, often with distinct and in some cases opposing interests. For example, trade and agriculture ministries may favour industry growth, sports and arts ministries may want tobacco sponsorship, and the finance ministry may believe its income from tobacco tax will fall. Only the health ministry is likely to firmly support the programme, and even here some health ministers may remain uncertain. (See also Chapter 12.)
- The theoretical enforcer is often a joint committee with the tobacco industry – and its powers are limited. The health ministry itself becomes a neutral party and cannot be an effective enforcer. In effect, it is like appointing a football team's best player as the referee.
- Unless legislation threatens, the tobacco industry may have little reason to observe the agreements.

The benefits of legislation

There is now a large and growing experience of effective legislation in many countries.

- Model control Acts can be obtained from WHO (and see Slama, 1998).
- The actual legislation can (and should) be relatively simple and general. The more complex and specific it is, the easier the tobacco companies' lawyers find ways round it.
- There must be substantial penalties for breaches of the legislation, e.g. fines must be very high indeed if they are to be real penalties for such rich companies; directors should be called to account (and if necessary punished) personally; a total ban on imports must be a possible sanction.
- The task of seeing that the legislation is carried out must be given to a particular government department. It must be responsible for prosecuting those who break the law.

Contents of a National Tobacco Control Act

The control of tobacco promotion

An effective policy will place a ban on all forms of tobacco promotion, direct and indirect. Direct promotion includes:

- press and poster advertising,
- advertising on radio, TV, cinema, video and audio tapes, the Internet etc.,
- sponsorship of arts and sport,
- commercial spots in cinemas,
- distributing free samples,
- gift coupon schemes,
- point of sale advertisements,
- public relations activities.

Indirect advertising includes all forms of promotion that are intended to advertise a tobacco brand but pretend to be something different. Sponsorship and 'brand stretching' are the commonest forms (see Chapter 9).

As one tobacco industry executive put it, 'Sponsorship is a form of advertising which enables us to introduce some glamour and excitement'. Tobacco companies often use sponsorship:

- as a way of getting round bans on direct advertising;
- to associate cigarette brands with a healthy or exciting sport, even where this is prohibited in regular advertising;

- to buy friends, by offering support to people who should be the allies of health, such as entertainment stars, sports stars (and their governing bodies), politicians – even scientists may be bought off if their research is sponsored;
- to buy public opinion, by funding sports, cultural events and entertainment and thereby inducing a fear for the future if tobacco companies no longer support them.

'Brand stretching' is a way of promoting a cigarette brand by selling other products with the same 'brand look' – name, typeface, logo, colours and so on. This strategy is most frequently used when direct advertising is banned, or seems likely to be banned. Examples are Camel boots and Marlboro or Lucky Strike clothing. Cigarette lighters are widely branded.

In some cases, 'front' organisations are created bearing the same name as a cigarette brand. For example, BAT is creating coffee shops in some African countries under the name 'Benson and Hedges'. Sometimes the spin-off company is a phantom. In Malaysia a heavily advertised 'holiday company ' with the name of a prominent brand turned out not even to provide tours.

'If it's a legal product'
The tobacco industry's favourite argument is that if the product is legal, it should be legal to advertise it too.

This argument is false. The fact that cigarettes are so widely available and advertised is something of a historical accident. If cigarettes had only just been invented, doubtless they would be universally banned. Tobacco had been grown and sold for many years before the dangers became known. In any case, there are many legal products, such as certain pharmaceuticals and toxic chemicals, which cannot be advertised, to protect the public.

The tobacco industry may also demand the right to continue to advertise so as to draw attention to allegedly less-dangerous 'low tar' cigarettes. But if all cigarettes are made low tar by central regulation, advertising will not be necessary (see below).

Why tobacco advertising must be banned
- It recruits young people to smoking. There is worldwide evidence that children are even more influenced by tobacco advertisements than adults. Countries that ban advertising tend to show a fall in children's smoking.
- It 'normalises' smoking, making it more socially acceptable.

- Ethics – governments should not allow the promotion of a product that is always highly dangerous, kills half its long-term users, and entraps children.
- It makes it harder for health education to convince people how dangerous tobacco is. Health advocates with minimal budgets have to fight against the tobacco companies' vast advertising resources. Smokers may say that if cigarettes really are as dangerous as they are told, governments would not let them be advertised or even sold.
- The immense amount of money that can be made from advertising cigarettes discourages its recipients (the mass media etc.) from publicising the dangers of tobacco.

There is now plenty of experience of how to introduce advertising bans, how tobacco companies try to get round them, and how to deal with the companies' arguments and obstructions.

Stimulated by tobacco companies, newspapers and magazines often fear loss of revenue. In practice, they have little to fear. Experience in Norway and elsewhere has shown that income from tobacco advertising is soon replaced by advertising of other products. See Appendix B for sources of help.

'I am a doctor. I believe in science and evidence. Let me state here today: tobacco is a killer. Tobacco should not be advertised, subsidised, or glamorised.'

Dr Gro Harlem Brundtland, Director General,
World Health Organization.

The importance of raising prices

Continually raising prices through increased taxation is one of the most successful ways of cutting tobacco consumption. Smokers are encouraged to stop smoking, and fewer young people start smoking. It does not even cut state revenues. Experience in many countries shows that, in general, a price rise of 10% results in a decrease in consumption of about 5% but an increase in total tax revenue of about 7%.

- Through taxation (including sales taxes, import duties etc.) the real price of tobacco must be increased in every annual national budget. This means the percentage increase must be greater than (a) the percentage increase in inflation and (b) the average national increase in personal income. (Figure 10.1.)
- The price rise must apply to all types of tobacco (manufactured cigarettes, hand-rolling tobacco etc.), to discourage switching.
- In some states (including California, USA, and Victoria, Australia) the government devotes some of this extra revenue to improving tobacco

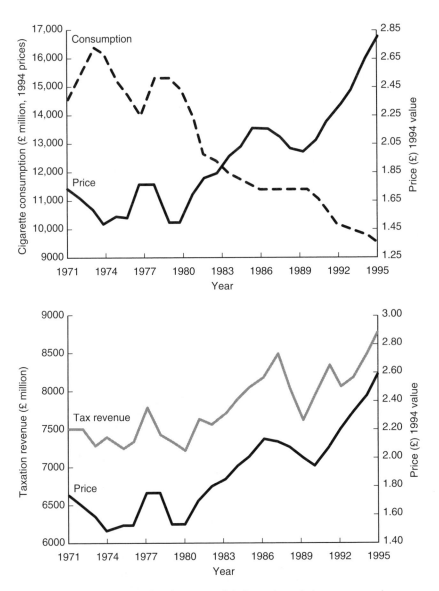

Figure 10.1 The relationship between (a) the price of cigarettes and consumption; and (b) between the price of cigarettes and tax revenue (1971–1996) in the United Kingdom. All variables are adjusted for inflation. (Adapted with kind permission from: Townsend. The role of tobacco taxation in tobacco control. In Abedian I et al. (eds). The economics of tobacco control. Cape Town, South Africa: University of Cape Town, 1998: 99)

control measures (e.g. health education, replacing tobacco sponsorship for sports or the arts).

■ In India, *bidis* (hand-rolled cigarettes enclosed in a leaf) are exempted from federal cigarette tax, because *bidis* are widely used by the poor. Two of the poorer Indian States have been exempted from federal tobacco tax in order to attract tobacco industry. These exemptions are liable to lead to massive abuse.

Control of smuggling

As discussed in Chapter 9, the decline in cigarette sales and the rise in tax revenues would be reversed if increased smuggling (and, to a lesser extent, bootlegging) led to a large number of contraband cigarettes flowing into a country. This can be countered by:

■ applying some of the increased tax income to strengthen the policing of cross-border traffic;
■ insisting that all cigarette packs carry health warnings in the local language or a stamp indicating that tax has been paid;
■ imposing severe penalties on convicted smugglers, including confiscation of their profits and destruction of their vehicles;

Figure 10.2 Tobacco tax increases should be regular.
(The above 'cartoon' has been reproduced by arrangement with The Economic Times and is the copyright of the publishers, Bennett, Coleman & Co. Ltd. The Economic Times may be viewed at http:\\www.economictimes.com.)

- maintaining extreme vigilance at national and international levels with regard to the possible involvement of the big tobacco companies in smuggling.

Indeed, there is much evidence that tobacco companies secretly cooperate with the distribution of cigarettes to criminal smuggling gangs. The Canadian government has sued several American tobacco companies for large sums to compensate for the damage smoking had done both to the health of Canadians and to Canadian government income.

Developing public education and information programmes

Public education consists of programmes aimed at specific target groups, such as school children and young adults (p 51), or women (p 42).

Public information acts chiefly through the news media. It seeks to provide a steady flow of accurate information about tobacco, both for the general public and to target groups such as politicians. It seeks to keep tobacco issues continuously before the public.

Public information and education frequently overlap.

Main objectives of public education and public information
- Make sure everyone knows that tobacco is very dangerous to health, both to smokers and others who breathe their smoke.
- Encourage in smokers the desire to quit.
- Support non-smokers in keeping off smoking.
- Ensure the right of non-smokers to enjoy smoke-free air.
- Promote non-smoking as the normal, natural and healthy behaviour.

Steps in public education programmes
- If your government does not yet have a commitment to tobacco control, you may have to start by working with a medical charity or some other national body that has some resources.
- Try to get some data about current smoking rates and attitudes to tobacco use in key target groups (e.g. children, adolescents, and pregnant women) (see Appendix A).
- Define the groups you need to target.
- Analyse the problems to be tackled.
- Design materials and a strategy for each target group.
- Train those who will deliver the programme.
- Test out on small sample groups. As a result of testing make any changes that seem necessary.

- Start delivering to the target group. For example, ask doctors to give a special leaflet to all smokers.
- Put in a system for evaluation (Appendix A). Do not expect a dramatic effect on smoking habits. Record this, but test how many have got your message. Record changes in attitude as a result of your programme. Evaluation can be done on just a sample.
- Remember successful programmes should be continued and reinforced over long periods of time, and varied to keep up interest.
- Take a long-term view. Don't be discouraged if change is slow. Advertising experts are pleased if a campaign for a product results in a market swing of just a few percentage points. Politicians often take a short-term approach. They like to sponsor something dramatic and showy that will appeal to voters. But test things first, and cancel if they do not prove effective. Replace unsuccessful programmes.

Free publicity
Save resources by getting free publicity, e.g. on state radio or TV channels. As a condition of licensing, private broadcasters may have to provide public service slots. These can be used for health programmes.

Public information
The main objectives are similar to those for public education, but public information is not so much a planned, researched programme like public education, but more a day-to-day operation to take advantage of events, to get accurate publicity about tobacco.

Catching media attention
Some basic tips on public information:
- Take every opportunity presented by public events, smoking-related illnesses of prominent persons etc. to reach large numbers through all news media.
- Learn how press and broadcasters work.
- Build up good relations with journalists and broadcasters. Make sure someone is always available (including in the evenings) to provide information and comment when there's an urgent need.
- Ensure that suitable experts are available to give interviews and to help journalists. Give them media training to improve their presentation skills.

Good activities include:
- Monitor and publicise tobacco companies' activities and reply to their propaganda.
- Argue the benefits of tax rises to secure public support.
- Discuss and support anti-tobacco activities.

- Promote the rights of non-smokers, and the need for smoke-free public places.
- Gather medical and scientific evidence against tobacco.
- Publicise ways of giving up use of tobacco.
- Track trends in tobacco consumption, including consumption by women, and publicise decreases in e.g. doctors, athletes, and teachers.
- Monitor government action (or inaction) on tobacco.
- Promote special non-smoking days or weeks such as WHO's World No-Tobacco day, and Quit-and-Win competitions.

Health warnings

The pack must become an advertisement for health. Strong effective health warnings, preferably with illustrations, should be compulsory on all tobacco packs (and on tobacco advertisements until these are banned). These should show the smoker the dangers of tobacco, and make clear the government's concern. The following points are important:
- The warnings should be on the top and front of the pack, covering at least 25% of each. Better still, aim to follow Canada's lead, with 50% coverage of each large side.
- They should be in the local language.
- There should be clear pictures or symbols for the less literate.
- They should give clear warnings about just how dangerous tobacco is – smokers usually do not realise the scale of the danger.
- They should give the tar and nicotine ratings (perhaps listed as 'Dangerous', 'Very Dangerous', or 'Highly Dangerous') and misleading terms such as 'Light' or 'Very Light' should be banned.
- Manufacturers should be required to rotate a series of warnings (perhaps 10 different at any one time). Smokers will then see all the warnings over a few weeks.
- Manufacturers should be required to enclose further anti-smoking information inside the package, perhaps in the form of 'anti-cigarette cards' or longer, illustrated health leaflets.

Some examples are shown in Figure 10.3.

Smoke-free zones

The aim here is to protect public health by ensuring public places are smoke free. Smoke-free areas should become the norm. Smoking should not be allowed in any indoor public places, except in designated smoking areas that must be physically isolated from the non-smoking sections. If workplaces are ventilated, separate systems should be installed if the fumes are not to be recycled to everyone. Smokers should not smoke in the doorways of clean air zones, since airflows mean much of their smoke will enter the building.

There are four major arguments for smoke-free public places:

- To protect children and non-smokers from risks to their health.
- To avoid the unpleasantness, smell and dirt of smoky rooms.
- To help to build up a climate of opinion that non-smoking is the more normal behaviour.
- Experience in the US and elsewhere shows smoke-free zones significantly reduce cigarette consumption by creating an environment that encourages smokers to quit and continuing smokers to smoke less.

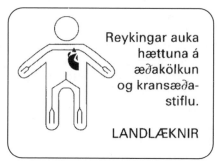

Smoking may damage your arteries and cause heart attack.

(a)

Smoking during pregnancy creates health risks for mother and child.
(b)

Figure 10.3 Examples of health warnings on cigarette packets in (a) Canada, and (b) Iceland. ((a) courtesy of Health Canada)

In many countries the idea that places should be smoke-free has begun to catch the public imagination. There is more and more pressure for clean air zones, and less resistance when such areas are suggested. Members of the public themselves may help enforce the bans, usually without generating conflict, but the management of the smoke-free places must take responsibility for enforcement.

Workplaces should always be smoke free, as non-smokers have no choice of avoiding exposure to smoke in them, if other workers are smoking. (Public places are usually also workplaces, of course.) Non-smoking workers have a right to be protected from smoke, and smokers often support this fact. Employers are also increasingly wary of legal action. Indeed, some have already faced manslaughter charges brought when a non-smoking worker has died, e.g. as a result of an asthma attack brought on by a co-worker's smoke.

Other desirable smoke-free areas include all health service premises, schools and universities, transport, offices open to the public, places of entertainment (including cinemas), and restaurants, bars and hotels.

At first, it may be necessary to provide small secluded areas for smokers positioned and ventilated so that the normal workplace is entirely free of smoke. These may be abolished later when no longer necessary.

Campaigning for smoke-free areas should be an important part of the anti-tobacco campaign. It has a major effect in helping people come to realise the dangers of tobacco smoke and the importance of quitting.

Reducing the toxicity of tobacco smoke

Tobacco manufacturers should be required to publish details of the ingredients in their cigarettes, including all additives, preservatives and flavourings, and the chemical composition of the smoke of each brand.

Governments should be able to regulate ingredients in detail, not just the tar and nicotine content but also carbon monoxide and other chemicals.

Testing must be carried out by a government laboratory, not by the tobacco industry, but the industry should be forced to pay, in return for the right to put the brand on the market.

But laboratory 'smoking machines', which test cigarettes, may mislead. The regular puffing on such machines does not accurately model how people actually smoke, and typically underestimates tar intake. For example, when smokers shift to 'low tar' cigarettes they tend to smoke more frequently, intensively and deeply to secure their accustomed dose of nicotine. They may also obstruct cigarette ventilation holes with their fingers. The result is that they take much more tar into their lungs than measurement by a smoking machine would suggest.

Upper limits

WHO suggests cigarettes should contain no more than 5–15 mg of tar. At present the European Union recommends that all higher tar brands should be steadily eliminated. Starting with eliminating all brands over 25 mg tar, this should be progressively reduced to 20, 15 and then 12 mg.

Some experts recommend low-tar, low-carbon monoxide, medium-nicotine cigarettes as the least dangerous. But American, Australian and British Medical Associations have jointly recommended their governments to make cigarettes less addictive by steadily reducing their nicotine to zero over the next 10 years. It is of course highly unlikely that anybody will become addicted to cigarettes, or continue to smoke, if there is no nicotine in them.

Support for quitting

We have covered desirable policies in this field in Chapter 7. Governments can give local health authorities guidelines and targets to be achieved. They can provide additional resources, e.g. out of the income from tobacco taxation.

Banning sales to children

The aim is to make it more difficult for children to start smoking. In many countries most smokers have begun to smoke in childhood. Successful bans might not only protect children, but reduce the number of adult smokers too. (In most countries, the definition of 'child' is someone under age 16 but in some it is 18.)

However there are problems with bans on sales to minors:

- The ban is often difficult to enforce. Police and other officials may not see it as a priority. It may be difficult to secure a conviction unless under-age children are observed buying tobacco. In some countries (e.g. Scotland), there are laws against 'enticement' and using underage children as 'test purchasers'.
- Children are further encouraged to see smoking as a sign of adulthood, and may regard buying cigarettes when under age as a desirable challenge.
- The tobacco companies often support banning sales to children – perhaps a sign that the companies think it will not be effective.

If bans are to be effective:

- It is the seller who must be prosecuted, not the child.
- Fines must be heavy. If shops have to be licensed to sell tobacco, breaking the law must lead to cancellation of that licence.
- The law should be monitored by local communities and monitoring bodies.

In spite of difficulties, the law on under-age sales is an important one. Even if not effectively implemented, it at least demonstrates society's intention.

Phasing out tobacco growing

Tobacco is grown commercially in more than 100 countries, 80 of them developing countries. Over the last 20 years production in high-income countries has fallen from 30% to 15%. Production in countries of the Middle East and Asia has risen from 40% to 60%, while Africa's share has grown from 4% to 6%.

The World Bank concludes that only two countries depend significantly on raw tobacco for their export earnings: Malawi with 61% of export earnings and Zimbabwe with 23%.

The Bank believes that action to reduce national tobacco production will have little effect on consumption (World Bank, 1999). Production will probably be increased elsewhere.

For many poor farmers in developing countries, growing tobacco can make obvious economic sense. For this reason, it is suggested that controlling the spread of tobacco farming should not have a high priority in tobacco control policy. Only as world demand decreases will governments need to provide help for these farmers to switch to other crops.

However the *subsidising* of tobacco crops by governments (as in the European Union) is a gross and immoral waste of resources. It should be phased out as soon as possible.

Implementing National Tobacco Control Programmes: lessons from the experience of various countries

International action

The desirable content of a national programme has been given in the box on page 96. A programme along these lines is likely to be incorporated in the proposed WHO Framework Convention on Tobacco Control (FCTC).

The publicity arising from the discussions leading up to FCTC's adoption by the World Health Assembly is likely to influence governments and public opinion in many countries to institute their national programmes. The task for anti-tobacco advocates is likely to become easier.

As we write, the European Union has agreed to phase out all tobacco promotion in the countries of the Union. There is some delay in implementing the law as the tobacco industry is challenging its legality through the European Union's European Court. This is an indication that the industry will desperately try to obstruct any law that might decrease tobacco use.

It is useful to be aware of some of the problems and opportunities that have arisen in countries that have adopted at least some items of a national programme.

Public opinion and legislation

- **Norway** and **Finland** were among the first countries to ban advertising and promotion of tobacco. In Norway, there was a notable fall in smoking rates during and immediately after the widespread discussion that led up to legislation. However, after the laws had been passed, discussion died away and taxation rates were not continuously raised. Smoking rates fell more slowly, evened out, and then tended to rise. Legislation had not been followed by continuing and intensive public education. This has since been remedied.
- In **Sweden** there has been a more continuous effort. A wide anti-tobacco alliance between public and voluntary bodies has had an on-going effect on public opinion. Currently Sweden has the lowest smoking rates in Europe. (On the other hand Sweden has an on-going tradition of using oral tobacco, an important public health problem, see Chapter 4.)
- In **Italy**, a number of admirable anti-tobacco laws were passed without fully arousing public opinion. As a result, few of the laws were fully and continuously implemented, though international tobacco companies have occasionally been fined or their imports briefly banned. We understand public opinion in Italy is now becoming more aggressive towards tobacco and the laws may become more effective.
- Similarly **France** has passed excellent laws well ahead of public opinion. Courts have imposed large fines on tobacco companies for breaking the law against tobacco promotion. But public opinion is not yet insisting that the law on smoke-free restaurant facilities is carried out in practice.
- In some states of the **USA** (notably California and Massachusetts), **Canada**, **Australia**, **Singapore** and **Hong Kong**, enthusiastic activists have successfully roused public opinion. Excellent legislation has been passed and is effectively implemented with strong public support.
- Some **Australian states** have pioneered using a proportion of increased tobacco tax to replace tobacco sponsorship of arts and sport. This has helped to keep public opinion 'on-side'.
- In the **USA**, litigation by tobacco-damaged patients, and by individual states seeking to recover health costs, has powerfully influenced public opinion. Tobacco companies have been forced to release secret documents revealing their ruthless policies. This has

greatly weakened the powerful tobacco lobby, making it easier for politicians to pass anti-tobacco laws, including the extension of smoke-free public places. For further details see Chapter 11.

Conclusions

■ The desirable content of a comprehensive national tobacco control programme is now generally agreed (p 96).
■ A number of countries are successfully introducing such programmes.
■ A model programme is likely to be incorporated in WHO's Framework Convention on Tobacco Control that countries worldwide will be asked to sign.
■ Making laws is easy. It's making them work that's the hard part. Anti-tobacco laws must be effectively implemented and monitored. A range of strong sanctions must be available to the courts.
■ A particular government department must be nominated to monitor implementation and prosecute those who break the law.

General references

Reid D. 1996. Tobacco control: overview. In Doll R, Crofton J (eds) Tobacco and Health. Br Med Bull 52(1): 108–120.
A useful review of the cost effectiveness of various measures, mainly based on British experience.
Slama K. 1998. Tobacco control and prevention. A guide for low income countries. Paris: International Union against Tuberculosis and Lung Disease.
A model Tobacco Products Control Act is given on pp 109–116.
US Departments of Health and Human Services. 2000. Reducing tobacco use: a report of the Surgeon General. Atlanta, Georgia: US Department of Health and Human Services, Centers for Disease Control and Prevention, National Center for Chronic Disease Prevention and Health Promotion, Office on Smoking and Health.
World Bank. 1999. Curbing the epidemic. Governments and the economics of tobacco control. Washington DC: The World Bank. ISBN 0–8213–4519–2.

11 | Tobacco and Legal Action

Litigation in courts of law both *by* and *against* tobacco companies has had a major influence in the fight against tobacco. Until recently, the tobacco companies nearly always won, which doubtless put a brake on progress. The turning point happened in 1996 when 'Big Tobacco' broke ranks and some companies began to admit to wrongdoing. Legal action, particularly in the USA, has since done much to publicise the extent of misconduct by the tobacco companies. Substantial damages amounting to billions of dollars have been agreed. Perhaps most importantly, it has forced the release into the open of millions of highly damaging secret industry documents.

Litigation by tobacco companies

For many years, legal action by tobacco companies has aimed to suppress the flow of information about the dangers of tobacco and prevent or delay tobacco control measures.

Tobacco companies often threaten libel action when advocates attempt to publicise industry misconduct. In practice, these threats often come to nothing, and there is no further action when the threat is ignored. Since the revelations in the US courts, threats of this sort are probably less likely now. Nevertheless it is wiser for activists to attribute any known misconduct to 'tobacco companies' or 'some tobacco companies' and not to name a particular company.

The industry always challenges the legality of proposed legislation. A current example is an attempt by the tobacco industry to have the European Court quash the European Union's ban on all forms of tobacco promotion.

Tobacco companies have used the legal system to oppose the regulation of the constituents of tobacco. In principle, nicotine (and some other ingredients of tobacco) should be treated like pharmaceuticals and regulated by governments in the interests of public safety – just as governments regulate food, alcohol, poisons and certain industrial chemicals.

So far the tobacco industry has managed to defeat any moves in this direction. For example, the industry persuaded the US Supreme Court that the Federal Food and Drug Administration should not be given powers to regulate nicotine.

In Sweden, a tobacco company took legal action against a tobacco control organisation for breach of copyright. A tobacco control booklet had included a copy of a tobacco advertisement clearly designed to influence the young. After legal action by the tobacco company, this had to be omitted from a later edition.

In the Netherlands, a tobacco company took action against a health organisation alleging misrepresentation of facts in an advertisement it was running about the dangers of environmental tobacco smoke (ETS). During the legal preliminaries the health organisation extracted industry documents confirming its claims. The industry then tried to withdraw its court action. However, the health organisation insisted on completing the court case and won. The industry had to pay all of the health organisation's legal expenses.

Litigation against tobacco companies

In recent years, the balance of legal action has shifted decisively the other way. Legal action against the tobacco industry has chiefly been taken by or on behalf of people whose health has been damaged by tobacco. Typically this has meant a group of patients bringing a 'class action' (which anyone with the same type of complaint can join) to seek personal compensation. Lawsuits have also been brought by health-care insurers, or by state and national governments, claiming compensation for the costs of treating smoking-related diseases.

A brief history of litigation in the USA

From 1954 to 1996 US patients fought a series of court actions none of which was successful. Tobacco companies successfully argued that health warnings on cigarette packets meant that the patients had freely chosen to smoke, or to continue to smoke, in spite of adequate warnings. Preposterous and hypocritical as this defence might sound, tobacco companies had endless resources to drag cases out, making the actions intolerably expensive for patients.

But things began to change when a number of US law firms agreed to take on cases on a 'no win, no fee' basis. Patients who have been long-term smokers have thereby won substantial compensation. This has sometimes also included additional, punitive damages for wrongdoing by the companies. In several cases, non-smoking workers (including flight attendants, bus drivers and office staff) who have fallen ill as a result of exposure to second-hand smoke have also won compensation from their employers.

Perhaps the most significant switch occurred in 1996 when one of the smaller US tobacco companies broke ranks with the rest of Big Tobacco and settled a case brought by several US states. The company agreed:

- to pay extensive damages;
- to add meaningful health warnings to cigarette packets;
- to provide testimony about industry misconduct for use in cases pending against other tobacco companies.

Subsequently, several US states and health insurance companies have won vast sums in compensation for the cost of treating smoking-related diseases. The tobacco industry is already committed to paying out US$10 billion each year. As part of the settlements, most outside advertisements for tobacco have now been banned. Many other cases are still pending.

In another trial, in Minnesota State, millions of previously secret industry documents were made public, revealing much about the industry's unscrupulous conduct over a very long period. This included:

- knowingly selling a lethal product, while claiming there was insufficient evidence of harm;
- systematically attempting to confuse and obscure the scientific evidence of damage done by cigarette smoke, including (most recently) ETS;
- denying nicotine is addictive, when secret industry research over many years had confirmed the opposite;
- chemically engineering cigarettes to increase the amount of nicotine absorbed by the smoker, making addiction speedier and more certain;
- using flavourings and other additives to make the flavour of cigarettes 'sweeter' and less harsh, making it easier for young people to take up smoking;
- failing to disclose the precise nature and purpose of the 600 or so additives present in cigarettes;
- failing to market 'safer (less lethal) cigarettes' – whether less hazardous to health because of reduced toxicity, or 'firesafe' cigarettes that extinguish themselves without causing fires;
- designing advertisements and other promotional strategies to attract children.

Litigation in other countries

At the time of writing, the governments of Venezuela, Bolivia, and British Columbia (Canada), and health insurers in Israel, are seeking

Figure 11.1 (Reproduced with kind permission of Tribune Media Services)

Figure 11.2 (Mike Smith © UFS. Reprinted by permission)

compensation from tobacco companies for health expenditure. A government health insurance organisation in France has won compensation.

In Bangladesh, health advocates got a court to ban BAT getting any publicity for a sailing boat promoting its cigarettes.

There have been a number of successful cases in Australia. In 1991 a Federal Court ruled that advertisements run in 1986 by the Tobacco Institute of Australia denying the ill effects of ETS had violated a Trades Practices Act that prohibits misleading or deceptive conduct in trade. Class actions on behalf of patients or states are pending.

A number of other countries, including several in South America, are suing in courts in the USA.

The future

In a country where successful litigation seems a possible ally in tobacco control, anti-tobacco groups may prepare by:

- calling meetings of relevant leading legal specialists;
- enabling doctors and other 'expert witnesses' to develop links with interested lawyers;
- publicising litigation matters to financial analysts and journalists – this will give on-going publicity to the dangers of tobacco and the wrongdoings of the tobacco industry.

Figure 11.3 (Reproduced with kind permission of Tribune Media Servies)

A huge range of incriminating industry documents has now become available in depositories in the USA and in England, and (most accessibly) on the Internet. The WHO is helping to analyse them for the benefit of health advocates. These will make it easier for patients or governments in other countries to take action.

Conclusions

■ In poor countries patients and tobacco control advocates may not be able to afford to challenge tobacco companies in court. But advocates can try to give maximum publicity to successful litigation in other countries. This will influence local public opinion against tobacco, and may prevent some local misconduct by the tobacco industry.
■ Publicity about tobacco industry misconduct means that litigation or threats of legal action against tobacco control organisations are now less likely. Nevertheless it is wise for advocates to avoid mentioning individual tobacco companies when making criticisms which could result in a libel action by the industry, unless there is sure proof.

General references

Daynard RA, Bates C, Francey N. 2000. Tobacco litigation worldwide. BMJ 320: 111–113.

Simpson D. 2000. Doctors and tobacco. London: Tobacco Resource Centre at British Medical Association. ISBN 0-7279-1491-X.

Up-to-date information on legal action can be found on the Tobacco Control Resource Center and the Tobacco Products Liability Project website (www.tobacco.neu.edu)).

12 | Campaigning

Without active campaigns, little if any tobacco control would ever be achieved. We have covered details of many aspects of campaigning (often called 'advocacy') throughout this book. In this chapter we briefly summarise these, and give cross-references to other chapters.

Campaigners often have to face various claims by the tobacco companies or their representatives. (The representatives sometimes conceal that they are speaking on behalf of the tobacco industry.) These claims mostly concern the dangers of tobacco or tobacco control measures. We summarise common questions and claims by tobacco interests and give the answers to these. Again we do this by giving cross-references to the pages where you can find more detail.

Finally we provide some examples of successful national campaigns.

Summary of campaigning issues

Campaigning issues are considered in answer to the following questions:
- **Why** must we campaign?
- **What** are we campaigning for?
- **Where** may we be campaigning?
- **Whom** are we trying to influence?
- **How** should we try to do the job?

WHY *must we campaign?*

- The main reason for campaigning is to prevent the sickness, misery and death resulting from tobacco. Half of all regular smokers will eventually die from a smoking-related disease (Chapter 2). Also many smokers become ill when they are young.
- Environmental tobacco smoke (breathing other people's smoke) can also cause illness and death (Chapter 3). Children are at particular risk (Chapter 6).
- Tobacco causes major economic loss, to patients and their families, to businesses, and to governments (Chapter 9, page 85).

WHAT are we campaigning for?

- We are campaigning for the control measures outlined in Chapter 10 (National Tobacco Control Programmes). These are summarised in the box on page 96.
- The most important points of these measures are:
- a ban on all tobacco promotion (Chapter 10);
- raising tobacco prices through taxation (Chapter 10);
- public education and information programmes (Chapter 10);
- strong prominent health warnings on tobacco packets (Chapter 10);
- smoke-free public places (Chapter 10);
- reducing toxicity of tobacco smoke (Chapter 10);
- support for smoking cessation (quitting) (Chapter 7);
- a ban on tobacco sales to children (Chapter 10);
- phasing out tobacco growing (Chapter 10);
- legal action, where relevant (Chapter 11);
- monitoring and evaluation of the campaign (Appendix A).
- The measures that are most likely to be most vigorously opposed by the tobacco industry are bans on all tobacco promotion, increased taxation, and the drive for smoke-free public places. This opposition shows how important these control measures are.

WHERE should we campaign?

- Many of these measures need national government legislation, so national campaigns are particularly important (Chapter 10).
- In large countries, regional government will be important (this includes states or provinces). This may be the appropriate level where you can best operate.
- Many advocates may have to start by building up action within local communities. They will seek action by local government authorities and local businesses.
- Finally, international action requires action by governments and international bodies. If you publicise in your own country what is happening internationally this may help you in national or local action. It will help to make your action more fashionable, more 'in tune with the times'. This will appeal to politicians and decision makers.

WHOM should we seek to influence?

- We are seeking to influence governments and decision makers.
- These people are influenced by public opinion.

- Public opinion is influenced by public education and public information (the box on page 103).
- We give a list of relevant opinion-leaders and organisations in the box below. You can add to this list from your local knowledge.

Important people and organisations to influence
- Politicians
- Health professionals
- Journalists, broadcasters
- Social workers and teachers
- Religious leaders
- Popular national figures, athletes, actors, singers etc.
- Non-governmental organisations (NGOs) and charities concerned with e.g. children, women, poverty
- Business leaders
- Trade union leaders

Below we give a few brief notes about some important opinion-leaders:

Politicians
It is always most effective to meet them personally. When some special legislation is coming before Parliament, try to organise letters to as many Ministers and politicians as possible from as many people as possible. Letters from health professionals and health professional societies are particularly effective (see Chapter 8). Try also to influence government officials who in turn may influence politicians.

Health professionals
Try to get all health professionals committed. See Chapter 8 regarding medical (and other) student education on tobacco issues and how health professionals can help. Include all main specialties, including dental workers, and not forgetting medical officers in the armed forces.

Journalists and broadcasters
Feed them information about important research advances; national statistics (e.g. smoking rate trends, death rates from tobacco etc.); evidence of misconduct by tobacco companies. Ensure that you can answer enquiries rapidly (including outside normal working hours) either personally or by passing them on to an expert; be prepared to react quickly to publicity concerned with tobacco, e.g. a tobacco-related illness in a public figure, new national statistics etc. Build up personal relations with media professionals. This will result in much free publicity (see Chapter 10). Remember that tobacco companies will be seeking to

have the opposite effect. But in many countries the media are now very much on the anti-tobacco side.

Social workers
Social workers are particularly important in poor areas where many people smoke. They need to be persuaded that they can tactfully help to reduce smoking, both in the community and by their individual clients. Both actions will reduce poverty.

Religious leaders
In many countries religious leaders can be very helpful, and often have influence over a wide range of people.

Popular national figures
Popular figures (e.g. sports stars, actors and actresses) can be very helpful in influencing the young.

Non-governmental organisations and charities
Non-governmental organisations and charities concerned with women (Chapter 5), children (Chapter 6) and poverty (many religious and social charities) need to be persuaded how much they can influence the climate of opinion among the groups they serve.

Business leaders
Business leaders may need to be persuaded how much sickness, absence and inefficiency are caused by tobacco. Smoke-free workplaces are more efficient. Some non-smokers have successfully sued employers for illness due to environmental tobacco. In many countries more and more workplaces are now smoke free.

Trade union leaders
Trade union leaders may have to be persuaded that they have a similar responsibility on behalf of their members. At first, they may take the tobacco industry's view about supporting tobacco-related employment. However, as they understand more about the problem, they will see that this view is not in the long-term interests of their members.

How to approach opinion leaders
We suggest you make a list of all the individuals and organisations you already have contact with, or think you could contact easily. Then list how, when, and by whom (if you are a working group) they will be contacted. Preferably, ask for a meeting to discuss your concern and to ask for help.

HOW to conduct campaigns

The possibilities will be very different in a country where public opinion and the government are still largely unaware of the threat of tobacco to health, compared with a country where a great deal has already been done. This book is mainly addressed to people in countries that have so far achieved less in tobacco control.

In such countries you will have to start increasing public awareness – particularly among opinion leaders. We have outlined some of the steps you can take in Chapter 10. We emphasise the value of forming an action group or committee – either national or local. This will often be started by doctors, consumer groups or health charities, but will then attract public-spirited advocates. It will become much more effective if it can employ staff who have continuous day-to-day responsibility. (Figure 8.1, p 75 shows the impressive drop in smoking rates in Great Britain after the foundation of such a committee, Action on Smoking and Health.) This basic committee can then build up alliances with health professional and other organisations, to form an ongoing alliance against tobacco.

Some examples of successful campaigning in various countries are given below.

Responses to anti-tobacco campaigns by the tobacco industry

Anti-tobacco advocates are an obvious threat to the profits of the tobacco industry. In the past the industry has sometimes tried to intimidate them by threat of legal action for libel. As we have pointed out in the last chapter, such threats are now less likely to result in legal action in Western countries. But the 'threat' might be used, even if it remains only a threat. See Chapter 11 for precautions against this.

Anti-tobacco activists may have to answer statements or claims by the tobacco industry, the advertising industry, or such industry-sponsored bodies as 'Smokers' Rights' or 'Freedom' organisations, over various aspects of tobacco control. Below we briefly list some of these, with cross-references to where in this book you can find the answers:

- Doubting the evidence for tobacco's effect on health, or claiming that 'more research is necessary'. For the overwhelming evidence about damage by active smoking, see Chapter 2. For the softening of the attitude of the industry, at least in the West, see Chapter 9. For environmental tobacco smoke (ETS), see Chapter 3.
- Claims that 'advertising does not increase consumption'. One scheme by the industry is to offer 'self-regulation' or 'voluntary agreements' instead of legislation. The tobacco companies always find ways of getting round any such agreements. Claims that the companies

should be able to advertise 'low tar' cigarettes, or 'safer' cigarettes. See Chapter 10.

- Claims that tax rises 'will increase *smuggling*', 'will particularly hit *the poor*', or 'will decrease *employment*'. See Chapter 10.
- Health warnings. The companies may use these as a defence against litigation. 'The smoker has chosen to smoke in spite of the warnings. The company is not responsible.' See Chapter 11, page 113.
- Banning sales to children. This is often supported by the industry, as it knows this measure is usually not effective in practice. See Chapter 6.
- 'We don't advertise to children'. Much evidence shows that they do. See Chapter 6.
- Tobacco control will damage national economies'. This has been firmly dealt with by a World Bank report. See Chapter 9.

Some examples of successful campaigns

Country A

In this country, so far there had been almost no tobacco control action. The international tobacco companies were using every type of advertisement and promotion. Smoking rates were going up, especially among the young, and some of the companies saw the country as a major base for exploiting the markets in the region.

However a consultant chest physician attending a conference overseas was asked by an international colleague to try to identify the most active anti-tobacco organisation in her country. She approached the main cancer, heart and lung associations, the health ministry, the national medical association and leading consumer groups. None of these was doing much nor were they keen to take the lead in campaigning for tobacco control. So the doctor herself decided to do this.

Over several years, while keeping in touch with colleagues overseas, she persuaded other doctors to join her in this work. They formed a committee. Taking advantage of the presence of international experts at a conference, they arranged a press conference to which a Member of Parliament (MP) was also invited. He had previously tried to initiate tobacco control legislation in the Parliament but had found little support. Encouraged by the strong interest of journalists at the press conference, he went straight back to Parliament and met its chairman ('Speaker') who agreed to give the Bill (the draft law) a chance to be debated.

The health group lobbied all MPs likely to support it and the Bill was passed. But to become law it still needed to be signed by the President. By this time the tobacco industry had started lobbying hard, including planting much misleading information in the press. The leader of the health group, with help from an international health agency, put an appeal on GLOBALink (for details see Appendix B), asking colleagues round the world to send faxes to the President. In due course the President invited the health group to visit him and assured them he would sign the Bill into law. This he duly did.

Country B

Several health groups, working on different aspects of tobacco control policy, noticed a major advertising campaign by a tobacco company. This campaign used a sailing boat travelling round the world to promote its cigarettes. The health groups raised the matter in letters to the press. This in turn resulted in more press coverage. A meeting was convened at which many health groups agreed to work together in an alliance to increase their lobbying power.

The proprietor of a national newspaper attended further meetings. This newspaper's editors had recently decided not to take tobacco advertising; to cover the tobacco issue from a health viewpoint; and to campaign for tobacco control measures. A lawyer from one of the health groups then approached the courts on behalf of the alliance. The court agreed to forbid the tobacco company from running advertisements covering the boat's progress. Later another judge issued an injunction forbidding newspapers and broadcasters from giving the story any further coverage. The increasing pressure on the government drew a promise to implement proper tobacco control legislation.

Country C

A local health group in a small town had good contacts with a prominent religious leader in the town. They realised he could be very helpful and asked to meet him, taking along a doctor who was a member of the health group. The religious leader was impressed by the weight of evidence about tobacco control and agreed to help. He preached to his congregation on the next holy day. This drew quite a large response.

A journalist among the worshippers reported it in the local newspaper. The local radio station then invited the religious leader and the doctor to come and talk on a current affairs programme. The religious leader attended a national convention the following month. He asked his colleagues to consider doing the same sort of thing. Inspired by the scale of the problem, on which the religious leader by now was something of an expert, it was agreed that on the nearest holy day to World Health Organization's World No Tobacco Day (31 May), each religious leader would preach about the importance of avoiding tobacco. They would encourage people not to start and encourage politicians to take action to protect future generations.

Country D

A sports journalist, whose brother had recently died from a smoking-related disease, was appalled to find that a tobacco company had become the major sponsor of his nation's sports journalists' association. The editor of his newspaper backed his decision to speak out about this. He wrote a column in the paper politely but firmly setting out the case as to why he thought this was wrong. A lot of publicity ensued, including defensive letters from the head of the sports journalists' association. There were comments on a popular radio programme, where listeners are encouraged to call in by telephone to give their views.

The cigarette company did not like the bad publicity it was getting over this cynical sponsorship. It postponed the annual event at which it had made a special award to athletes. This in turn created further publicity. The sports journalists' association was put under pressure to find another sponsor. By this time the Ministry of Health had taken a position to discourage this sponsorship. Politicians raised the question in Parliament. Leading athletes said that they would refuse to go to a tobacco company's event. The health group contacted GLOBALink (see Appendix B). Messages of support for them came from around the world. Another sponsor came forward to replace the tobacco company.

Country E

A foreign tobacco company proposed to set up a local factory to produce a new form of oral (sucking) tobacco designed to appeal to the young. The factory was to receive government support. It was to be opened with wide publicity, including television. A senior dentist heard of this proposal. He contacted a local anti-tobacco group. They organised a demonstration by dentists, doctors and health advocates outside the factory on its opening date. They had informed the media who attended in force. The tobacco company publicity programme was cancelled.

Later a group of local mothers lobbied local shops and persuaded them not to sell the new product to their children. Later still, the women sent a delegation to the Prime Minister's office, with full publicity. As a final result of this and much else the product was banned in the whole country. This was followed by a ban in many neighbouring countries.

Conclusions

Remember that the effects of campaigning will be slow. They very much depend on the gradual development of public opinion (see Chapter 10). However, much is now happening in many countries and internationally. The climate is becoming more favourable. Action on tobacco is becoming more fashionable with politicians. But remember we still have a powerful enemy in the tobacco industry. It is still very, very far from being defeated.

References

Mackay J, Crofton J. 1996. Tobacco and the developing world. Br Med Bull 52(1): 206–221.
    Includes a brief history of the tobacco industry's activities, especially related to Asia.
Pollock D. 1996. Forty years on: a war to recognise and win. How the tobacco industry has survived the revelations on tobacco and health. Br Med Bull 52(1): 174–182.
    Mainly an account of how a major multinational company has successfully avoided tobacco control for such a long time.
Simpson D. 2000. Doctors and tobacco. London: Tobacco Control Resource Centre at British Medical Association. ISBN 0-7279-1491-X.
Sweda EL Jr, Daynard RA. 1996. Tobacco industry tactics. Br Med Bull 52(1): 183–192.
    Mainly recounts tobacco industry tactics in the USA.
World Bank. 1999. Curbing the epidemic. Governments and the economics of tobacco control. Washington DC: World Bank. ISBN 0-8213-4519-2.
    An excellent and readable report. Very useful to quote.

APPENDIX A
Model Questionnaires

Questionnaires on tobacco use

Globally available data on smoking prevalence have been published by WHO (1997) and by the World Bank (1999). We have summarised some of this material in Chapter 1.

Understandably, politicians, administrators and the general public will be most influenced by statistics from their own community. To carry out a national survey of smoking habits in a country it is best to consult a statistician. The statistician will advise about the choice and size of the sample to be questioned.

For local surveys of a smaller population you may be able to get some idea of the size of the local problem, and save on cost, by carrying out a survey using older schoolchildren or students to do the work. The children can record the smoking habits of the adult members of their families. (For this purpose 'an adult' would be aged 15 years or over.) Remember to record gender. Of course the results would only give you an approximate idea; but they may be sufficient to affect local leaders and start local action.

It is general experience that the more questions you ask the less accurate the answers. If you can only ask one question, we suggest: Do you now smoke daily, occasionally or not at all?

If you can ask more questions, we suggest that you use the International Union against Tuberculosis and Lung Disease (IUATLD)/Amended WHO Core Questionnaire: cigarette smoking (Questionnaire 1, below) (Slama, 1998).

Where smokeless (oral) tobacco is used extensively, we suggest that you use the similar Amended WHO Core Questionnaire: smokeless tobacco (Questionnaire 2, below).

Questionnaire 1 IUATLD/Amended WHO Core Questionnaire: cigarette smoking

Age _____   *Gender* _____   *Residence* _____   *Education level* _____
Marital status: _____   *Occupation* _____   *Religion* _____

Q1   Have you ever smoked at least 100 cigarettes or the equivalent amount of tobacco in your lifetime? (Y/N).

Q2   Do you now smoke daily, occasionally or not at all? (D, O, not at all)

Q3   **If you have ever smoked, on average, what number of the following items do/did you smoke per day?** (Include only the items commonly used in your locality)

___ manufactured cigarettes

___ hand-rolled cigarettes

___ bidis

___ pipefuls of tobacco

___ cigars/cheroots/cigarillos

___ goza/hookah

Q4   At what age did you start smoking? ___ years

Q5   If you have stopped smoking completely, how long has it been since you last smoked?

___ less than one month

___ one month or longer but less than six months

___ six months or longer but less than one year

___ one year or longer

Q6   At what age did you stop smoking completely? ___ years

Questionnaire 2 Amended WHO Core Questionnaire: smokeless tobacco

Age _____   *Gender* _____   *Residence* _____   *Educational level* _____
Marital status: _____   *Occupation* _____   *Religion* _____

Q1   Have you ever used smokeless tobacco? (Y/N).

Q2   Have you used smokeless tobacco at least 100 time in your lifetime? (Y/N).

Q3   Have you ever used smokeless tobacco daily? (Y/N)

Q4   Do you now use smokeless tobacco daily, occasionally or not at all? (D, O, not at all)

Questionnaire 2 *(continued)*

Q5 **If you have ever used smokeless tobacco, on average, what number of the following items do/did you use per day?**
(Include only the items commonly used in your locality)

___ snuff (oral use)

___ snuff (nasal use)

___ chewing tobacco

___ betel quid

Q6 At what age did you start using smokeless tobacco? ___ years

Q7 If you have stopped using smokeless tobacco completely, how long has it been since you last used it?

___ less than one month

___ one month or longer but less than six months

___ six months or longer but less than one year

___ one year or longer

Q8 At what age did you stop smoking completely? ___ years

Notes on the questionnaires
- Residence: If possible give this or, alternatively, some other indication of socio-economic level (e.g. poverty or greater prosperity). If this is too difficult, omit this item.
- Educational level: E.g. no school education, primary education only, secondary education, tertiary education (college or university).
- Religion: Only include if this is important and useful in that community.

The IUATLD book on Tobacco Control and Prevention (Slama, 1998) provides samples of other more extensive questionnaires.

Surveys on the tobacco habits and knowledge of health professionals can be helpful for two reasons:
1. To give you basic information. This can help you decide what needs to be done (a) to change habits if smoking rates are high (b) to improve undergraduate and post-graduate education if the survey shows important ignorance about certain items.
2. The survey is likely to stimulate interest in the subject among the professionals. If the survey is of students of a health profession, it is likely also to stimulate the interest of their teachers. (See Chapter 8, p 79.)

Questionnaire 3 (Global Health Professional Survey) is the latest from WHO, prepared in consultation with IUATLD.

Questionnaire 3 WHO Global Health Professional Survey

Date (month/yr.)   Code (country, city)

DEMOGRAPHY

Q1)   What is your gender?   1. Female   2. Male   ☐

Q2)   What is your age?   ☐☐

Q3)   What is your nationality? _____

Q4)   Are you a: 1. Doctor   2. Nurse   3. Dentist
        4. Other (specify) _____   ☐

Q5a) What is your speciality _____

Q5b) Do you have contact with patients?   1. Yes   2. No   ☐

CIGARETTE USE

Q6)   **Which of the following best describes your smoking behaviour?**
        1.   **I have never smoked cigarettes** → *Go to Q15*   ☐
        2.   I have quit smoking → *go to Q12*   ☐
        3.   I currently smoke occasionally (Some days) → *Go to Q7*   ☐
        4.   I currently smoke every day → *Go to Q7*   ☐

┌──┐
│   **If you** CURRENTLY *smoke*   │
└──┘

Q7)   How old were you when you first started to smoke on a
        regular basis?   Age ☐☐

Q8)   What brand of cigarettes do you smoke most frequently? (list one)
        _____

Q9)   *On the days that you smoke,* how many cigarettes do you smoke
        per day? (**Give average number**)   # ☐☐

Q10) Have you ever stopped smoking for at *least one week*?   ☐
        1. Yes   2. No

Q11) Which of the following best describes how you feel about your
        smoking?
        1. Not ready to quit within the next 6 months → **Go to Q15**
        2. Thinking about quitting within 6 months → **Go to Q15**   ☐
        3. Ready to quit NOW → **Go to Q15**

┌──┐
│   **If you smoked in the** PAST   │
└──┘

Q12) When you smoked in the past, how often did you smoke?
        1. Daily (Every day)   2. Occasionally (Some days)   ☐

CIGARETTE USE (continued)

Q13) How old were you when you first started to smoke on a
   regular basis?   Age ☐☐

Q14) How old were you when you stopped smoking completely? Age ☐☐

USE OF OTHER TOBACCO PRODUCTS

Q15) How often do you use the following tobacco products **Nowadays**?

> **Please use the following codes where applicable:**
> **1. Daily**   **2. Occasionally**   **3. Never**   **4. Not applicable**

Shisha_____ ;   Pipes_____ ;   Cigars_____ ;   Bidies_____ ;
Nasal snuff_____ ;   Chewing tobacco_____ ;   Oral snuff_____ ;
Betel quid_____   Other (specify)_____ ;

KNOWLEDGE AND ATTITUDES

For Q16 to Q37 refer to cigarette smoking. Please use the codes below:
1. Strongly Agree   *2. Agree*   *3. Unsure*   *4. Disagree*
5. Strongly Disagree

Q16) Smoking is harmful to your health.   ☐

Q17) Health professionals serve as role models for their patients
   and the public.   ☐

Q18) Health professionals should set a good example by not smoking.   ☐

Q19) Patient's chances of quitting smoking are increased if a health
   professional advises him or her to quit.   ☐

Q20) Health professionals should routinely ask about their patients
   smoking habits.   ☐

Q21) Health professionals should routinely advise their smoking
   patients to quit smoking.   ☐

Q22) Health professionals who smoke are less likely to advise people
   to stop smoking.   ☐

Q23) Health professionals should get specific training on cessation
   techniques.   ☐

Q24) Health professionals should speak to lay groups about smoking.   ☐

Q25) Smoking in enclosed public places should be prohibited.   ☐

Q26) Health warnings on cigarette packages should be in big print.   ☐

Q27) Tobacco sales to children and adolescents should be banned.   ☐

KNOWLEDGE AND ATTITUDES (continued)

Q28) Sport sponsorship by tobacco industry should be banned. ☐

Q29) There should be a *complete* ban on the advertising of tobacco products. ☐

Q30) Hospitals and health care centres should be 'smoke-free'. ☐

Q31) The price of tobacco products should be increased sharply. ☐

Q32) Neonatal death is associated with passive smoking. ☐

Q33) Maternal smoking during pregnancy increases the risk of Sudden Infant Death Syndrome. ☐

Q34) Passive smoking increases the risk of *lung disease* in non-smoking adults. ☐

Q35) Passive smoking increases the risk of *heart disease* in non-smoking adults. ☐

Q36) Paternal smoking increases the risk of lower respiratory tract illnesses such as pneumonia in exposed children. ☐

Q37) Health professionals should routinely advise patients who smoke to avoid smoking around children. ☐

WORKSITE PRACTICE

Q38) Where is your workplace/practice located?
1. Urban   2. Rural   3. Suburban   4. Not applicable ☐

Q39) What sort of smoke-free policy is in place at your workplace?
1. No smoking policy in place → **GO TO A41** ☐
2. Smoking rooms available → GO TO Q40 ☐
3. No smoking allowed at all on the premises → GO TO Q40 ☐

Q40) Is the smoke-free policy enforced?
1. Yes: always   2. Yes: sometimes   3. No   4. Don't Know ☐

Q41) Are following interventions **AVAILABLE** to YOU to help your patients stop smoking?

Please use the following code:	1. Yes	2. No	
a Traditional remedies?	1. Yes	2. No	☐
b Self-help materials	1. Yes	2. No	☐
c Counselling	1. Yes	2. No	☐
d Medication (Nicotine gum, patch, buproprion)	1. Yes	2. No	☐
e None	1. Yes	2. No	☐
f Other (specify) _____			

WORKSITE PRACTICE (continued)

Q42) Which of the following interventions do you **USE** to help your patients stop smoking?

	Please use the following code:	**1. Yes 2. No**	
a	Traditional remedies?	1. Yes 2. No	☐
b	Self-help materials	1. Yes 2. No	☐
c	Counselling	1. Yes 2. No	☐
d	Medication (Nicotine gum, patch, buproprion)	1. Yes 2. No	☐
e	None	1. Yes 2. No	☐
f	Other (specify) _____		

Q43) How well prepared do you feel you are when counselling patients on how to stop cigarette smoking?
1. Very well prepared.
2. Somewhat prepared
3. Not at all prepared.   ☐

Q44) Have you ever received any formal training in smoking cessation approaches to use with your patients?

	Please use the following codes:	**1. Yes 2. No**	
a	Formal training during medical school		☐
b	Formal training during post-graduate programs		☐
c	Special conferences, symposia or workshops		☐
d	Other explain _____		

Q45) What could WHO do to support your efforts to reduce smoking among your patients in your community?

_____

_____

_____

_____

---

* REGULAR means at least one cigarette a day for daily smokers and at least one cigarette a week for occasional smokers.
Reprinted by permission of WHO.

References

Slama K. 1998. Tobacco control and prevention. A guide for low income
countries. Paris: International Union against Tuberculosis and Lung
Disease. ISBN 2-9504238-6-8.
As well as core questionnaires on smoking and smokeless (oral)
tobacco this book gives a list of possible additional questions on ages
of starting smoking, health knowledge, smoking behaviour, readiness
to stop, and questionnaires on 'social perception of tobacco use' and
an extensive combined questionnaire on these subjects. You can
obtain copies of these questionnaires from the International Union
against Tuberculosis and Lung Disease, 68 Boulevard Saint-Michel,
75006 Paris, France.

World Bank. 1999. Curbing the epidemic. Governments and the
economics of tobacco control. Washington: World Bank.
ISBN 0-8213-4519-2.
An excellent, short and readable account of the world tobacco
situation. Covers global and regional trends in tobacco use, health
consequences, and the economics both of tobacco and of tobacco
control.

World Health Organization. 1997. Tobacco or health. A global status
report. Geneva: WHO. ISBN 92-4-156184-X.
A thorough review of global consumption, smoking rates, tobacco
industry and national tobacco control action by country up to
1995–96. Mainly valuable as a reference book.

APPENDIX B
Sources of Further Help

Canada

Research for International Tobacco Control (RITC) (a Secretariat housed at the International Development Research Centre)
250 Albert Street
P O Box 8500
Ottawa, Ontario, CANADA, K1G 3H9
Contact: Ms Rosemary Kennedy, Coordinator
Tel: +1 613 236 6163
Fax: +1 613 236 4026
Email: ritc@idrc.ca
Website: www.idrc.ca/tobacco

France

International Union against Tuberculosis and Lung Disease (IUATLD)
68 boulevard Saint-Michel
75006 Paris 6ᵉ
FRANCE
Contact: Dr Karen Slama (kslama@worldnet.fr)
Tel: +33 1 44 32 03 60
Fax: +33 1 43 39 90 87
Website: www.iuatld.org

The Tobacco Section of IUATLD works very closely with INGCAT (International Non-Governmental Coalition against Tobacco).

International Non-Governmental Coalition against Tobacco (INGCAT)
P O Box 23244 Joubert Park
2044 Johannesburg
SOUTH AFRICA
Contact: Dr Karen Slama (kslama@worldnet.fr)
Tel: +27 11 720 6177
Fax: +27 11 720 6177
Email: info@ingcat.org
Website: www.ingcat.org

This is an international coalition of, mainly, international non-governmental organisations. They work together mainly on campaigning issues. They produce a newsletter for associate members, including many in developing countries.

Hong Kong

Asian Consultancy on Tobacco Control
Riftswood, 9th Milestone
DD 229, Lot 147
Clearwater Bay Road, Sai Kung
Kowloon, HONG KONG
Contact: Professor Judith Mackay
Tel: +852 2719 1995
Fax: +852 2719 5741
Email: jmackay@pacific.net.hk

This is an important source of information, both factual and on campaigning issues, for Asia and Western Pacific.

Switzerland

GLOBALink
International Union Against Cancer
4 rue du Conseil-General
1205 Geneva
SWITZERLAND
Contact: Ruben Israel
Tel: +41 22 809 1850
Fax: +41 22 809 1810
Email: israel@uicc.org
Website: www.globalink.org

This is the main international Internet site and closed conferencing and email communications system for tobacco control advocates on both factual and campaigning issues.

International Union Against Cancer (UICC)
3 rue du Conseil-General
1205 Geneva
SWITZERLAND
Tel: +41 22 809 1811
Fax: +41 22 809 1810
Email: info@uicc.org
Website: www.uicc.org

United Kingdom

International Agency on Tobacco and Health (IATH)
Tavistock House
Tavistock Square
London WC1H 9LG, UK
Contact: Professor David Simpson
Tel: +44 20 7387 9898
Fax: +44 20 7387 9841
Email: admin@iath.org

IATH is a non-governmental organisation that provides an information and advice service, including a detailed monthly information bulletin, to tobacco control colleagues in countries with fewer resources.

Tobacco Control: An International Journal
BMJ Publishing Group
Journals Marketing Department
PO Box 299
London WC1H 9JR
UK
Contact: Sarah Coulston, Marketing Executive
Tel: +44 20 7383 6486
Fax: +44 20 7383 6661
Website: www.tobaccocontrol.com

Tobacco Control Resource Centre
c/o British Medical Association
50 Thistle Street Lane North East
Edinburgh EH2 1DA
UK
Contact: Sinéad Jones, Project Leader
Tel: +44 (0) 131 247 3072
Fax: +44 (0) 131 247 3071
Email:tcrc@bma.org.uk
Website: www.tobacco-control.org

Concerned with all countries in the WHO European Region and of particular interest to countries in Central and Eastern Europe.

Cochrane Tobacco Addiction Group
ICRF General Practice Research Group
Division of Public Health and Primary Care
Institute of Health Sciences
Old Road, Headington
Oxford OX3 7LF, UK

Contact: Mrs Lindsay Stead, Coordinator
Tel: +44 1865 226997
Fax: +44 1865 227137
Email: lindsaystead@dphpc.ox.ac.uk

This group is part of the Cochrane Collaboration, which prepares, maintains and promotes the accessibility of systematic reviews of the effects of health care. Abstracts of reviews on different methods of smoking cessation by the Tobacco Addiction Group are at: www.cochrane.org/revabstr/ g160index.htm

ASH (Action on Smoking and Health)
102–108 Clifton Street
London EC2A 4HW, UK
Contact: Deborah Arnott, Director
Tel: +44 20 7739 5902
Fax: +44 20 7613 0531
Email: action.smoking.health@dial.pipex.com
Website: www.ash.org.uk

Mainly concerned with the UK but has an international section which could be helpful.

TALC (Teaching-aids At Low Cost)
PO Box 49, St Albans
Hertfordshire AL1 5TX, UK
Contact: David Chandler
Tel: +44 1727 853869
Fax: +44 1727 846852
Email: talc@talcuk.org
Website: www.talcuk.org

Teaching-aids At Low Cost (TALC) is a non-profit organisation that supplies teaching aids and books to raise standards of health care worldwide. TALC is professionally advised by the Centre for International Child Health at the Institute of Child Health, London. Over the last 30 years TALC has distributed 7 million transparencies with text and over a million books, largely to Africa.

United States of America

Office on Smoking and Health
National Center for Chronic Disease Prevention and Health Promotion
Centers for Disease Control and Prevention (CDC)
Mail Stop K-50
4770 Buford Highway NW, Atlanta
Georgia 30341-3724, USA

Contact: Dr Samira Asma
Tel: +1 770 488 5487
Fax: +1 770 488 5939
Email: sea5@cdc.gov
Website: www.cdc.gov/nccdphp/osh/tobacco.htm

A major source of world epidemiology figures and progress of the anti-tobacco campaign in various countries.

World Bank
Centers for Disease Control and Prevention
Health, Nutrition and Population
Room S-9065
1818 H Street, NW
Washington, DC 20433, USA
Contact: Joy de Beyer, CDC Liaison
Tel: +1 202 458 7617
Fax: +1 202 522 3489
Email: jdebeyer@worldbank.org
Website: www.worldbank.org

A major source for information on all economic aspects of tobacco.

Advocacy Institute
1629 K Street, NW,
Suite 400
Washington, DC 20006-1629, USA
Tel: +1 202 777 7575
Fax: +1 202 777 7577
Website: www.advocacy.org

Mainly concerned with USA but has an international interest, especially in training.

International Network of Women Against Tobacco (INWAT)
PO Box 224
Metuchen
New Jersey 08840
USA
Contact: Ms Bonnie Kantor, Secretariat
Tel: +1 732 549 9054
Fax: +1 732 549 9056
Website: www.inwat.org

INWAT is a network dedicated to supporting and uniting women in actions to prevent tobacco use among women. INWAT's three major objectives are to counter the marketing and promotion of tobacco to women, to develop programmes that help girls and women to resist starting or to give up smoking, and to promote women's leadership in the tobacco control movement.

World Health Organization

Tobacco Free Initiative (TFI)
World Health Organization
Avenue Appia 20 1211
Geneva 22
SWITZERLAND
Contact: Project Manager
Tel: +41 22 791 2108
Fax: +41 22 791 4832
Email: tfi@who.int
Website: www.who.int/toh

This is the office of the central, international WHO programme on tobacco.

WHO Regional Advisors for Tobacco Control
Regional Office for the Americas:
World Health Organization
Regional Office for the Americas/Pan American Health Organization
(AMRO/PAHO)
525, 23rd Street, NW
Washington, DC 20037
USA
Contact: Dr Bryna Brennan, Chief DPI
Tel: +1 202 974 3457
Fax: +1 202 974 3143

Regional Office for Europe:
World Health Organization
Regional Office for Europe (EURO)
8, Scherfigsvej
DK-2100 Copenhagen 0
DENMARK
Contact: Peter Anderson, Regional Advisor, TFI
Tel: +45 3 917 13 36
Fax: +45 3 917 18 80

Regional Office for Africa:
World Health Organization
Regional Office for Africa (AFRO)
Parirenyatwa Hospital
PO Box BE 773
Harare
ZIMBABWE

Contact: Mr S. Ajibola, INF
Tel: +263 4 70 69 51/70 74 93
Fax: +263 4 70 56 19/70 20 44

Regional Office for the Eastern Mediterranean:
World Health Organization
Regional Office for the Eastern Mediterranean (EMRO)
WHO Post Office
Abdul Razzak Al Sanhouri Street
(opposite Children's Library)
Nasr City
Cairo 11371
EGYPT
Contact: Adil Salahi, Regional Advisor, TFI
Tel: +20 2 670 2535
Fax: +20 2 670 2492/2494

Regional Office for South East Asia:
World Health Organization
Regional Office for South East Asia (SEARO)
World Health House
Indraprastha Estate
Mahatma Gandhi Road
New Delhi 110002
INDIA
Contact: Mrs Harsaran Bir Kaur Pandey, Information Officer
Tel: +91 11 331 7804/7823
Fax: +91 11 331 8607

Regional Office for the Western Pacific:
World Health Organization
Regional Office for the Western Pacific (WPRO)
PO Box 2932
1000 Manila
PHILIPPINES
Contact: Dr Seppo Suomela, Public Information Officer
Tel: +63 2 528 9984
Fax: +63 2 521 1036

Index